Longman Practice Exam Papers

A-level Psychology

Mike Cardwell

Series editors:

Geoff Black and Stuart Wall

Titles available for A-Level

Biology
Business Studies
Chemistry
Physics
Psychology
Pure Mathematics and Mechanics
Pure Mathematics and Statistics

Addison Wesley Longman Limited
Edinburgh Gate, Harlow
Essex CM20 2JE, England
and Associated Companies throughout the World

© Addison Wesley Longman 1999

The right of Mike Cardwell to be identified as author of this work has been asserted by him in accordance with the Copyright, Designs and Patents Act 1988.

All rights reserved; no part of this publication may be reproduced, stored in any retrieval system, or transmitted in any form or by any means, electronic, mechanical, photocopying, recording, or otherwise without either the prior written permission of the Publishers or a licence permitting restricted copying in the United Kingdom issued by the Copyright Licensing Agency Ltd, 90 Tottenham Court Road, London W1P 9HE.

First published 1999

ISBN 0-582-36923-1

British Library Cataloguing in Publication Data
A catalogue record for this book is available from the British Library

Set in Times 11/13 and Gill Sans by 38

Printed in Singapore

Contents

Glossary of AEB terms   v
Marking criteria: AEB A/AS-level psychology   vii
Editor's preface   viii
Acknowledgements   viii

Practice exam papers
Module Paper 4 (Social and comparative psychology)   1
Module Paper 5 (Biopsychology and atypical development/abnormal behaviour)   2
Module Paper 6 (Cognitive and developmental psychology)   3
Module Paper 7 (Perspectives and research methods)   4

Solutions to practice exam papers
Module Paper 4   6
Module Paper 5   18
Module Paper 6   32
Module Paper 7   45

How to use this book

- This book is designed to help you prepare for your GCE A and AS-level Psychology examinations. The questions are set at the same standard, using the same rules of question setting, as in the actual examinations.
- These questions are based on the AQA (AEB) A and AS-level Psychology examinations, although they will also be helpful for the OCR and AQA (NEAB) examinations.
- The layout of the practice exam papers covers all four written modules of the AEB examination, and all the subsections within those modules. You may not have covered all of these subsections, so don't be surprised if some of the questions look unfamiliar.
- If you are following an AEB modular examination route, you are required to answer **two** questions from Module 4, **two** from Module 5 and so on. As these essays cover only one possible question from each subsection, make sure that you can also answer other possible questions within that subsection. When in doubt, ask your teacher.
- All questions are designed to be answered in about 40 minutes. A very valuable exercise is to plan each essay in the form of eight paragraphs, with each paragraph representing about 100–120 words and about five minutes' writing. That way you can ensure that you are addressing all parts of the question and that you are allocating the correct amount of time to each.
- Within the AEB marking criteria, marks are divided between Skill A (knowledge and understanding) and Skill B (commentary). Each of these is indicated within a question by a Skill A or Skill B injunction. These are included in the glossary on page v. Make sure that you can recognise them and structure your answer appropriately. Remember that Skill A is worth 12 marks and Skill B is worth 12 marks – no more, no less; so make sure your answers are balanced across these two skills.
- You might like to try a selection of the questions from this book. Try doing them under examination conditions, and then use the marking criteria on page vi to get an idea of the marks you would have received. As a rough guide, if you get around 17 or above, then your answer would be worth a grade A (provided the rest of your exam performance is as good).
- Each question has been answered for you within the body of the book. Remember that these are *sample* answers for *these specific questions*, not model answers, and should be used as such. Your own answers, using quite different material, could be every bit as good (perhaps better) as these and should, of course, be tailored to the exact requirements of the question set. Each of these answers, mostly written by me, but with the occasional good student essay thrown in, would be good enough to get that elusive grade A mark.

- All the answers are around the 1000-word mark and could be written in the 40 minutes provided in an examination for one essay. I have tried to stick to my eight paragraphs rule outlined earlier. This certainly does make the writing of examination answers more systematic and therefore easier.
- There is help in the interpretation of all the questions. Often what lets students down in an examination is that they misinterpret examination questions and lose marks through carelessness. All examination questions require very careful reading, as it is all too easy to misinterpret what they require (as I remember all too well from my own A-level English Literature exam).
- Most important, stay positive. It is never too late to start revision. If you feel you have underperformed in any of these areas, simply spend time revising that topic and try again. Remember you are simply acquiring a skill. If you aren't very good, practise until you get better. If you have bought this book yourself, it shows you are motivated, which is good. If your parents bought it for you, that's even better. It shows they love you, which may be very important in the months to come!

Using these practice exam papers

In this book there are four Module Papers, based on the AEB A-level syllabus. They have been given the same module numbers as the AEB exam (Modules 4–7), although students following the AEB linear route would take the same papers, with Modules 4 and 5 being their Paper 2, and Modules 6 and 7 being their Paper 3. My apologies to NEAB and OCEAC students, but these essays should still be useful for these syllabuses as well.

- Module Paper 4 (Social and comparative psychology): Two questions, $1\frac{1}{2}$ hours
- Module Paper 5 (Biopsychology and atypical development/abnormal behaviour): Two questions, $1\frac{1}{2}$ hours
- Module Paper 6 (Cognitive and developmental psychology): Two questions, $1\frac{1}{2}$ hours
- Module Paper 7 (Perspectives and research methods): One essay question and (usually) two research methods questions, $1\frac{1}{2}$ hours

Sample answers are given in the second part of the book. Do remember that these are only **sample** answers to **these specific questions**. Try to write your own answers to these questions, but above all, remember that these answers are only effective because they are addressing the specific requirements of the question set. That is what you **must** do in an examination, or you will be disappointed with your examination results.

Glossary of AEB Terms

Skill A terms

Consider: Show knowledge and understanding of the topic area. This is achieved not only by what is presented, but also by the way in which it is presented, how arguments are constructed and developed.

Define: Explain what is meant by a particular term. These do not have to be textbook definitions, but may be your own.

Describe: Show knowledge of a topic area. It is always followed by the content requirement in the question, e.g. 'Describe two theories of ...' or 'Describe research studies into ...'.

Examine: Provide a detailed descriptive account of a topic area. This may be treated as the same as 'describe'.

Explain: Show understanding of a topic through coherent and intelligible explanation. This invites more than just simple definition.

Outline/State: Offer a summary description of the topic area. The content does not have to be elaborated in quite the same detail as for 'describe'.

Skill B terms

Analyse/Critically analyse: Show understanding by examining the different components of a topic area. For example, a theory might be analysed by looking at the degree to which it is supported by evidence, or is internally consistent.

Assess/Critically assess: Present a considered appraisal through a review of the strengths and weaknesses of the information presented, or the value of a topic area.

Criticise: Evaluate in terms of the strengths and weaknesses of the topic area. Note that this requires *both* strengths *and* weaknesses.

Evaluate/Critically evaluate: Make an informed judgement as to the value of an argument, theory or piece of research.

Justify: Consider the grounds for a decision, e.g. in the choice of a particular statistical test.

Skill A + B terms

Compare and contrast: Consider both the similarities and the differences between two topic areas.

Critically consider: Show knowledge and understanding of the topic area, as well as its strengths and weaknesses.

Distinguish between: Consider the differences between two topic areas. This is not unlike 'compare and contrast', but is restricted to demonstrating only the differences between areas.

Discuss: Describe and evaluate a topic area (see definitions above for these terms).

Other terms

Concepts: An idea or group of ideas. These are often the basic units of a model or theory.

Evidence: Material that might be drawn from either theories or investigations and is used to support or contradict an argument or theory.

Findings: The outcome or product of *research* (see below).

Insights: Perceptions from theories or investigations that enable us to understand or appraise a topic area.

Methods: Different ways in which empirical research is and may be carried out.

Model: A term that is used synonymously with 'theory', although it may refer to something that is less elaborate or complex.

Research: The process of gaining knowledge, either by an examination of appropriate *theories* or through *empirical* data collection.

Studies: These are *empirical* investigations.

Theory: A set of interrelated ideas or principles that can be used to explain observed phenomena.

Marking Criteria Used in AEB A/AS-Level Psychology

Skill A Assessment Criteria

Band	Marks	Content (Knowledge, description and understanding)	Relevance	Construction and organisation	Breadth and depth
1 (bottom)	0–2	Just discernible/anecdotal/inaccurate	Wholly or mainly irrelevant		
1 (top)	3–4	Basic, rudimentary, sometimes flawed	Sometimes irrelevant		
2 (bottom)	5–6	Limited, generally accurate but lacking in detail		Reasonable	Some evidence of breadth and/or depth
2 (top) depth	7–8	Limited, although accurate and reasonably well-detailed		Reasonable	Increasing evidence of breadth and/or
3 (bottom)	9–10	Slightly limited, although accurate and well-detailed		Presented coherently	Evidence of both but imbalanced
3 (top)	11–12	Appropriate: accurate and well-detailed		Presented coherently	Substantial evidence of both and appropriate balance between them

Skill B Assessment Criteria

Band	Marks	Commentary (Skill B content according to injunction)	Use of material	Elaboration
1 (bottom)	0–2	Just discernible although weak, muddled and/or incomplete	Wholly or mainly irrelevant	
1 (top)	3–4	Minimal, superficial and rudimentary	Restricted	
2 (bottom)	5–6	Reasonable but limited	Reasonably effective	Some evidence of elaboration
2 (top)	7–8	Reasonable but slightly limited	Effective	Evidence of coherent elaboration
3 (bottom)	9–10	Informed and appropriate	Effective	Evidence of appropriate selection and coherent elaboration
3 (top)	11–12	Informed and thorough	Highly effective	Evidence of appropriate selection and coherent elaboration

Skill D (Quality of Language) Assessment criteria

Band	Marks	Expression of ideas	Use of specialist terms	Grasp
1	0	Poor	Limited range	Poor
2	1	Adequate	Good range	Adequate
3	2	Accurate	Precise/broad	Only minor errors

Editors' preface

Longman Practice Exam Papers are written by experienced A-level examiners and teachers. They will provide you with an ideal opportunity to practise under exam-type conditions before your actual school or college mocks or before the A-level examination itself. As well as becoming familiar with the vital skill of pacing yourself through a whole exam paper, you can check your answers against examiner solutions and mark schemes to assess the level you have reached.

Longman Practice Exam Papers can be used alongside *Longman A-level Study Guides* and *Longman Exam Practice Kits* to provide a comprehensive range of home study support as you prepare to take your A-level in each subject covered.

Acknowledgements

This book is dedicated to my daughter Alex, who makes a mean cup of coffee.

Mike Cardwell

Longman Examination Board

General Certificate of Education: Advanced Level
Module Paper 4: Social and Comparative Psychology

Answer two questions, one from each section

Time: 1½ hours

Section A:

1. Discuss the nature and role of social representations. **(24 marks)**

2. Discuss research relating to the effects of interpersonal relationships (e.g. on happiness and mental health). **(24 marks)**

3. Describe and evaluate research into obedience. **(24 marks)**

4. Discuss the view that the media may have a *pro-social* effect. **(24 marks)**

Section B:

5. Discuss the effects of predator–prey and symbiotic relationships on the evolution of behaviour patterns. **(24 marks)**

6. Discuss the nature and consequences of sexual selection in evolution. **(24 marks)**

7. 'Why do animals live in groups?'
   Critically consider the role of sociality in non-human animals. **(24 marks)**

8. Describe and evaluate **one or more** explanations of foraging behaviour. **(24 marks)**

Longman Examination Board

General Certificate of Education: Advanced Level

Module Paper 5: Biopsychology and Atypical Development/Abnormal Behaviour

Answer two questions, one from each section

Time: 1½ hours

Section A:

1. Discuss research into the effects of any **two** drugs on behaviour. **(24 marks)**

2. Describe and evaluate **two** methods used to investigate cortical functioning. **(24 marks)**

3. Describe and evaluate **two** theories of dreams. **(24 marks)**

4. (a) Outline and evaluate **one** physiological theory of motivation. **(12 marks)**

   (b) Outline and evaluate **one** non-physiological theory of motivation. **(12 marks)**

Section B:

5. Describe and evaluate research relating to the causes and effects of any **one** emotional or behavioural problem in childhood (e.g. attention-deficit hyperactivity disorder or autism).
(24 marks)

6. (a) Describe **either** the DSM **or** ICD approach to the definition and classification of normal and abnormal behaviour. **(12 marks)**

   (b) Evaluate this approach in terms of its practical problems and ethical implications. **(12 marks)**

7. Describe and evaluate social/psychological explanations of **two** anxiety disorders.
(24 marks)

8. (a) Describe **one or more** psychodynamic therapies. **(12 marks)**

   (b) Assess the appropriateness and effectiveness of this approach/these approaches for the treatment of psychological disorders. **(12 marks)**

Longman Examination Board

General Certificate of Education: Advanced Level
Module Paper 6: Cognitive and Developmental Psychology

Answer two questions, one from each section

Time: 1½ hours

Section A:

1. Describe and evaluate constructivist and direct explanations of perception. **(24 marks)**

2. Describe and evaluate experimental studies of selective (focused) attention. **(24 marks)**

3. Discuss applications of memory research. **(24 marks)**

4. Describe and evaluate **two** theories of the relationship between language and thought. **(24 marks)**

Section B:

5. Discuss research into cross-cultural differences in child-rearing and the effects of such differences. **(24 marks)**

6. Describe and evaluate **two** theories of cognitive development. **(24 marks)**

7. Describe and evaluate **two** theories of gender role development including the evidence on which they are based. **(24 marks)**

8. Describe and evaluate research into the impact of life events in adulthood. **(24 marks)**

Longman Examination Board

General Certificate of Education: Advanced Level

Module Paper 7: Perspectives and Research Methods in Psychology

Answer one question from Section A and all the questions in Section B

Time: $1\frac{1}{2}$ hours

Section A:

1. Discuss the importance of reductionism in explanations of human behaviour. **(24 marks)**

2. With reference to **either** psychological theory **or** research, discuss the view that such practices offer a gender-biased view of human behaviour. **(24 marks)**

3. Discuss the ethical issues of socially sensitive research. **(24 Marks)**

Section B:

4. Medicine often throws up many innovative ways of helping people recover from surgery. One such technique popularised in recent years has been 'pet therapy' where patients are given regular access to dogs, rabbits and other small animals as part of the recuperation process following surgery. Psychologists studied children on two children's wards; one in a hospital that subscribed to the pet therapy scheme and one that did not. Results suggested that those children who were allowed regular contact with pets made a more rapid recovery after surgery compared to those who were not.

    (a) Explain **one** advantage and **one** disadvantage of natural experiments such as this.
    (4 marks)

    (b) Investigations involving children involve special ethical issues. Explain **two** ethical concerns that might apply to this study. **(4 marks)**

5. Psychologists were interested in the effects that music might have on workers carrying out simple computational tasks. They chose to study examination board script checkers, whose job it is to check that all the addition of marks is correct. In one room, script checkers completed two one-hour sessions of checking specially prepared scripts, the first in silence and the second with the accompaniment of piped music. In another room, a second group of script checkers, matched for age and experience with the first group, completed the same task, but in the reverse order (a process known as counterbalancing). Participants recorded all errors on a separate document, noting every time an addition error occurred.

    The investigators awarded one mark for each script error correctly identified by the script checkers. The scores for the two groups are summarised in Figure 1.

    A Wilcoxon signed ranks test was carried out on the data. The value of T (65) obtained was non-significant at the 5% significance level ($p > 0.05$), but significant at the 10% level ($p < 0.10$).

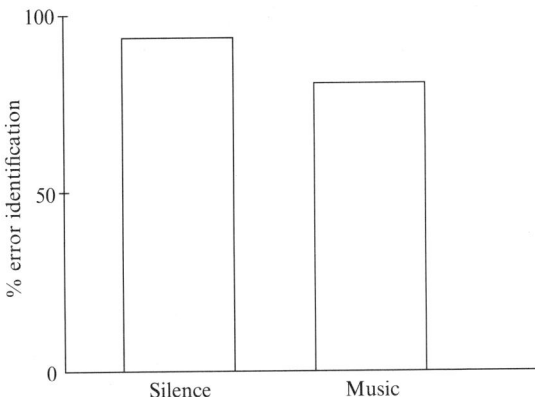

Figure 1: Summary of error identification scores for silence and music groups

(a) State an appropriate non-directional (two-tailed) hypothesis for this investigation.
(2 marks)

(b) State the independent variable in this study. **(1 mark)**

(c) Explain **one** factor relating to the choice of music that the investigators would need to consider when planning this study. **(2 marks)**

(d) The investigators chose a matched-participants design for this study. Describe **one** advantage of this method. **(2 marks)**

(e) Explain the purpose of counterbalancing in this investigation. **(2 marks)**

(f) Name the graphical technique shown in Figure 1. **(1 mark)**

(g) Give **three** reasons why the Wilcoxon signed ranks test was used for this investigation.
(3 marks)

(h) Explain what is meant by the statement 'The value of T (65) obtained was non-significant at the 5% significance level ($p > 0.05$), but significant at the 10% level ($p < 0.10$).'
(3 marks)

Solutions to practice exam papers

Module Paper 4

Section A

1. Discuss the nature and role of social representations. (24 marks)

> **TIP**
>
> There is an actual topic area called social representations theory, so don't be tempted to answer questions like this unless you actually do know something about the area. All too frequently, students who haven't studied this area try to fit pre-prepared answers on prejudice, conformity or any other area of social psychology in the vain hope that it might be relevant. Note that the question asks for the *nature* (what they are) and the *role* (how they are used) of social representations. The injunction is 'Discuss', so you will be required to offer some sort of critical evaluation of the content as well.

The theory of social representations is normally associated with Serge Moscovici (1981), who defines social representations as being a 'set of concepts, statements and explanations that originate in daily life in the course of inter-individual communication. They are the equivalent in modern society of the myths and belief systems of traditional societies, or may even be seen as the modern equivalent of common sense.' Social representations are a way of organising and simplifying information from our complex social environments, essentially a way of turning the unfamiliar into the familiar. Traditional social representations may become progressively removed from their social origins. For example, the Protestant work ethic was originally found among cultural groups that contained a high proportion of Protestants. Now the social representation of 'hard work as a virtue' has become detached from its origins in a particular religious group.

Moscovici suggested that the simplification role of social representations is achieved through the processes of anchoring and objectification. By 'anchoring', Moscovici means the process by which unfamiliar ideas are classified and integrated into categories and images that are already familiar. This is principally achieved through the medium of language, and the names and labels we use to describe unfamiliar objects and ideas (e.g. 'mad', 'foreign'). By including an unfamiliar object or event into a familiar category, we remove it from the realm of the strange, bizarre and hence potentially frightening; it now becomes part of *our* world (Slugoski, 1998). By anchoring unfamiliar objects and ideas into familiar categories, it enables us to make further inferences based on that category membership.

The process of objectification involves the conversion of ideas that are initially complex or abstract into images that are more concrete or familiar. Through this process, we find ways of making an idea easier to grasp so it can be used in daily discourse. Metaphors and similes are an important part of this process as they enable us to relate an unfamiliar idea to a concrete image that we already possess. Objectification can happen in a number of ways. A whole economic doctrine can be objectified by linking it with one person – 'Thatcherism', or a belief in the origins of humankind as 'Darwinism'. This process is known as personification. Alternatively, a metaphor may be used to describe ideas such as ecological awareness as 'green', a process known as figuration (Hayes, 1997).

Together, these processes define what we perceive as common sense, our representation of the world and how it works. Moscovici further stresses that the process of social representations is both implicit and coercive. Once formed, our social representations are rarely questioned and provide the background assumptions and expectations about the world without which it would be extremely difficult to function. Social representations set limits on what we are able to conceive, because once we have used anchoring and objectification to define an object or idea, it becomes extremely difficult to conceive it any other way (Slugoski, 1998). The coercive nature of social representatons lies in their ability to mould the way we think about an object and the actions we might take towards it. For example, if we represent a group of people (a group of football fans, for example), as 'animals', our social representation of fans as 'animals' means that we would subscribe to treatment that involves 'herding' and 'caging' as natural consequences of the label.

Durkin (1995) argues that child development is also something about which we have distinct social representations. An obvious consequence of social representations in this context is that they influence the way we raise and educate the young. The term 'intelligence' for example, is represented by many as a natural 'thing' possessed more by some than others. It is believed by many educators to be genetically determined which, in turn, affects they way they approach the education of 'intelligent' and 'unintelligent' children. This is a pervasive social representation, and one that has sinister social implications, especially when applied to equally controversial representations of 'race'. Belief in an inherited difference between groups can blind people to other possible explanations and can be used to support divisive and discriminatory social policies.

To study social representations within a cultural group, we need to look at all instances of communication among members of that group. However, the theory does not specify in advance how one might 'select' members of the group. Moscovici specifies only that the group *is* the people who hold a shared social representation, a form of circular reasoning. For example, DiGiacomo (1980) studied Belgian university students who were involved in a protest about student grants. The representations held by the leaders of the protest (e.g. the principle of student–worker solidarity) were at odds with the representations held by the student body. As a result, when leaders called for action by the student body, there was very little support for it (Gross and McIlveen, 1998). One cannot conclude, therefore, that social representations are consensual. Groups, and likewise individuals, can differ as to the content of their social representations of the same object or event.

Social representations theory also fails to specify the level at which social representations are formed, and whether the processes of anchoring and objectification take place at an intra-individual level or an interindividual level. Furthermore, there appear to be major differences in the types of social representation found in different cultures. For example, representations of 'illness' appear to be different in individualistic and collectivistic cultures. Presenting symptoms in the former are frequently linked to 'feelings' of anxiety or depression, whereas in the latter they tend to be more 'physical'. A final criticism of the theory is that the mechanisms of social representations are somewhat conservative, as they have the role of transforming the novel and unfamiliar into the familiar and reassuring (Manstead et al., 1995), an essentially passive relationship between science and the society in which it operates.

2. Discuss research relating to the effects of interpersonal relationships (e.g. on happiness and mental health). **(24 marks)**

> **TIP**
>
> This question is making a number of specific requests, and also offering some suggestions on suitable content. You are asked to discuss (i.e. describe *and* evaluate) research (this can be from either empirical investigations or theories) into the effects (not the causes) of interpersonal relationships. It is easy to lose track of exactly what the question has asked you to do, so careful reading of the question is essential. The examples in brackets are just that, examples. You may choose to write about the effects of relationships in quite different areas. This is an area that invites personal anecdotes and subjective assertions. Try to avoid the temptation to offer your own personal insights into life and relationships, no matter how interesting your own personal experiences have been in this area. Marks are available for psychology, and that's what you should attempt to deliver.

There are many different forms of interpersonal relationships, each of which has been shown to have some positive effects on psychological well-being. These include marriage or partnering, family, friends and neighbours. The positive effects of these relationships can be experienced through the development of emotional attachments with others (and therefore exposure to caring and empathy), help and social support, affirmation through positive evaluation by others, and the provision of confidants with whom we may disclose and discuss our personal problems and concerns. The importance of all of these for psychological well-being has been amply demonstrated by psychological research, and I will highlight some of that research evidence in this essay.

Probably the most important relationship to us as adults is when we form a lasting relationship with a spouse or life partner. Argyle and Henderson (1985) provide support for this statement with their research finding that 'falling in love' was seen as the most important factor in the happiness of adult respondents. An experiment by Reich and Zautra (1981) also lends support for this assertion. Subjects were asked to increase their involvement in positive events (such as starting a love affair, joining a club or finding new friends). At the end of the month, subjects reported significant increases in their overall outlook on life, and an improvement in their general psychological well-being. This improvement was particularly pronounced in subjects who had undergone a string of negative experiences prior to the study, demonstrating the 'remedial' effects of interpersonal relationships. Although this study clearly highlights the importance of interpersonal relationships in the predicted direction, it is best not to read too much into its findings. In common with many 'experiments' in social psychology, the subjects were aware that they were taking part in a psychological study, and would therefore be more susceptible to demand characteristics in their reporting of any changes in outlook that took place as a result of their involvement in the study. It is also highly likely that subjects were drawn from a student population, where relationships are made more easily and are more transitory in nature.

Probably the most persuasive evidence for the power of relationships in our overall level of happiness comes from studies of people who have lost a spouse through death or divorce. A significant finding in this field is that from Morgan (1980) who discovered that widowed men were far less happy than married men of the same age, and were far more likely subsequently to die compared to the psychologically better protected married men. The period immediately following the death of a spouse is the most significant for men, with a sharp increase in the death rate during this period. Men are also far more likely to commit suicide during this period, with a falling-off in both the death rate and the likelihood of suicide in the period beyond the first six months after the event. The incidence of physical illness is also greater for those who lose a spouse through death or divorce, with far more widowed and divorced people taking significant periods off work compared to those who are still married or who have stayed single (Bloom et al., 1980). This is also true for mental illness, with a higher incidence of widowed and divorced people showing evidence of mental disturbances (usually depression) after the loss. However, this assumes a particular direction in the results obtained, i.e. that the depression was a result of the loss, when it is also possible that whatever disorder is observed (e.g. depression or alcoholism) is the cause of the loss (in the case of divorce) rather than its consequence. Bloom (1978), in an attempt to discover which came first, the loss or the depression, found evidence for a causal effect in both directions.

A second major source of psychological well-being is the presence of a social support network. Social support can be experienced through friends, work colleagues or even children. Research evidence has shown that physical and mental health are better for those with well-developed social networks of this type than for those without. For example, DiMatteo and Hays (1981) found that kin and friends have significant effects on the physical and emotional recovery of patients who have undergone serious operations, or are recovering from serious illness. It has also been demonstrated (Turner, 1981) that social relationships have a significant effect on the prediction of later psychological disturbances. Those with weak or relatively non-existent social networks are more likely to experience later psychological disturbances than those who have well-developed networks of kin, friends, etc. However, the existence of psychological problems such as depression can also be an indication of later social isolation, so it is difficult to disentangle the effects of one upon the other. Indeed, evidence from Brown and Harris (1978) has shown that far from being a source of social support, children can actually be a source of considerable stress, and are more likely to contribute to feelings of isolation and depression in certain people if adequate adult support is not available.

Recent research has complicated the relationship between social support and the development of psychological disturbances. Henderson and Duncan-Jones (1985) have shown that it is the perception of social support as being inadequate that has the greatest link with the development of neurotic mental illness. Likewise, too much help from others may reduce self-reliance, and distract attention from the real cause of the problems. It is clear, therefore, that relationships may have negative as well as positive effects on the psychological well-being of the individual, and that the relationship itself may be the major source of stress.

3. Describe and evaluate research into obedience. (24 Marks)

> **TIP**
>
> This is a very straightforward and 'friendly' question that offers you the chance to unload all that you know about obedience to authority. This 'friendliness' may well be your undoing, because many students can't resist the opportunity to fill their answers with fairly tedious procedural detail, and miss the really insightful content. Sometimes questions ask specifically for the 'findings' from research in this area, so it would pay you to invest a bit more time in considering what researchers have *found* rather than what they have *done*. You should also be clear what is and what is not 'obedience'. Milgram's research definitely *is* relevant, and Asch's conformity research definitely is *not*. Hofling and Zimbardo are often included but can you think *why* they are examples of obedience, rather than offering them blindly as representative research in this area? Note that you are also being asked to *evaluate* research. You will probably include some of the accusations levelled at Milgram regarding the ethics of his research, but what about his responses to those criticisms? You may also like to consider whether the experimental deception actually worked, and whether similar results are found in other cultures.

Obedience refers to a type of social influence whereby somebody acts in response to a direct order from another person. There is also the implication that the actor is made to respond in a way that the actor would not otherwise have done without the order. The most famous experiments in this area were carried out in the US by Milgram in the 1960s. Milgram deceived 40 male volunteer subjects into thinking they were giving gradually increasing electric shocks to other subjects during a word association task. In the baseline condition, the 'learner' was in another room, with no voice contact with the 'teacher'. Of the 40 subjects, all continued to at least 300 volts, and 65% continued to the full 450 volts.

Milgram extended his research to explore the different situational factors that led subjects to obey or not to obey. He discovered that the closer the subject was to the teacher, the more likely they were to refuse the experimenter's command. Milgram also discovered that obedience levels were lower when the experimenter was not physically present and gave orders over the phone. In a reversal of the original condition, Milgram found that when the learner insisted on the continuation of the shocks (to show he could take it), *all* subjects obeyed the experimenter immediately when he gave the order to stop giving shocks.

Baumrind (1964) has criticised the ethics of Milgram's research. One criticism is that subjects were prevented from giving their informed consent to take part in the study. As a result of studies like Milgram's, the APA now insist that experimenters give subjects more information before they take part in a study.

Milgram answered these criticisms by providing evidence of the stress shown by his subjects, and self-reports by subjects who believed that they *had* been giving real shocks. In a repetition of the experiment in run-down office buildings, Milgram found that the percentage of subjects who obeyed up to 450 volts was still very high (50%).

Milgram's research demonstrated that obedience was a much more pervasive phenomenon than was previously thought. Replications of the basic study in other countries (e.g. Australia, Germany and Jordan) provided support for the suggestion that obedience to authority is a universal phenomenon. However, Smith and Bond (1985) suggest that these studies differ from Milgram's in important ways (e.g. the nature of the subjects and the nature of the task, and cultural differences in the perception of scientific investigations) that limit their usefulness as direct comparisons. APA ethical restrictions have prevented replications of Milgram's study so that direct comparison cannot be made.

A second criticism is that participation in the study could have long-term effects. Subjects might have suffered lowered self-esteem because of what they had done and developed a future distrust of authority figures. Milgram argued that debriefing after the experiment was sufficient to get rid of these negative feelings, and this was supported in a follow-up survey. Milgram has defended the study by suggesting that the study has provoked controversy because of the *results* rather than the procedures used to gain them.

The validity of the experiments has been criticised by Orne and Holland (1968). Orne and Holland claimed that the study lacked both internal validity (i.e. the subjects did not believe they were really giving electric shocks) and external validity (the results were only obtained because the experiment took place within the lab of a prestigious American university).

In the light of Milgram's findings, psychologists have explored *why* people obey. First, those in authority relieve others of their responsibility for their actions. In Milgram's experiments, as in many real-life examples, subjects believed they were only obeying orders, and therefore were not directly responsible for any consequences. Second, people obey those with badges or uniforms, or other indications of status and power. Research by Bushman (1988) showed that when an accomplice of the experimenter was dressed in a uniform, people were more likely to obey their 'commands' to give money to somebody who needed it for a parking meter. Third, people are likely to obey large-magnitude orders when the initial command is quite small and the increase in magnitude is gradual.

Research has also focused on how people can resist obedience. Three main findings have been obtained. First, individuals can be reminded that it is they who are responsible for their actions, not the authority figures. Hamilton (1978) found that under these conditions, sharp decreases in obedience could be obtained. Second, the presence of *disobedient* models (which might suggest that obedience is inappropriate) can serve to reduce obedience. Finally, there is growing evidence that knowledge of results such as Milgram's enhances people's ability to resist destructive obedience.

Research such as Milgram's has changed the way in which we view the nature of destructive obedience. Prior to this research, it was traditional for social scientists to explain behaviour such as Nazi war crimes in terms of deviant personalities. The current view is that destructive obedience may be evoked in the majority of people purely by situational factors. The capacity for moral decision-making is suspended when an individual is embedded within a powerful social hierarchy. This has led some to comment on the 'ordinariness' of such evil acts rather than seeing them as the product of pathological personalities (Arendt, 1963).

4. **Discuss the view that the media may have a *pro-social* effect.**

(24 marks)

> **TIP**
>
> Again, this appears to be a very straightforward question, as indeed it is. However, when this was first asked at AEB A-level, most candidates wrote either a general essay on pro-social behaviour, or an essay on the anti-social effects of the media. Of course, none of us would make that mistake, but rather like commentators on Milgram's obedience research, we all tend to think that *we* would be different. You should try to include as much actual research and as little personal speculation. It is easy to make claims about the beneficial effects of *Sesame Street*, but is there any research evidence for these effects? The injunction 'Discuss' lurks in the background in this question, so you should ensure that whatever content you are including, there is a critical component to it as well.

There is increasing evidence that good behaviour shown on television can have positive influences on the behaviour of children watching. Some studies have investigated specially prepared programmes such as *Sesame Street* and *Mister Rogers' Neighbourhood*. Freidrich and Stein (1975) found that children as young as four who watched episodes of *Mister Rogers' Neighbourhood* where people tried to understand and help a stranger, displayed more helpful and co-operative acts in their own behaviour afterwards. Psychologists believe that examples of pro-social behaviour on screen will not only lead to increased pro-social behaviour among watchers in similar real-life situations, but will also be generalised to other situations as well. Zielinska and Chambers (1995) found that exposure to videotaped parts of *Sesame Street* among day care children led to increased pro-social behaviour afterwards (compared to children who had seen segments with no pro-social content), but only if the children were given the opportunity to rehearse the behaviours they had seen on screen.

Despite the evidence that these specially constructed pro-social programmes can have powerful effects, they remain somewhat contrived and artificial and may not be generalisable to the normal television viewing material of most children. Popular television dramas have also been studied.

Rubenstein et al. (1975) studied five- and six-year-olds. In one condition, subjects watched an episode of *Lassie* in which a boy risks his life to save a puppy. In the other two conditions (another episode of *Lassie* and an episode of the family comedy *The Brady Bunch*) there was no such example of altruistic behaviour. As a result, those who had watched the first episode were more likely to respond to (fictional) puppies in distress and for longer than the other two conditions. Although this suggests that showing a pro-social behaviour on screen can lead to the reproduction of that behaviour in real life, the two acts were very similar. What this does not show, however, is whether watching pro-social acts has an effect on dissimilar behaviours. In another study, Murray et al. (1977) found that preschool children exposed to a four-week 'diet' of either 'pro-social' or 'neutral' programmes showed subsequent differences in general 'sociability' after the conclusion of the study. Those who had watched programmes with a high pro-social content showed an increase in helpfulness and co-operation despite the fact that the behaviours demonstrated by the children were quite different from the behaviours shown by the central characters in the programmes watched.

As with the study of the alleged anti-social effects of the media, a major criticism of these studies is that they do not adequately represent the normal viewing conditions of the watching children. Surveys of the viewing habits of children have shown a higher correlation between exposure to violent television and aggressive behaviour than between exposure to pro-social television and subsequent pro-social behaviour. However, there are reasons for this difference. First, children learn very early on in their socialisation about sharing and helping others, therefore television merely repeats what they already know. Aggressive behaviour, on the other hand, is generally regarded as undesirable and wrong, and seeing it on television – especially if used by the central characters – contrasts with that message. Second, aggressive acts on television are normally blatant and physical, thus having a higher visual impact, and consequently are more memorable. Pro-social behaviours, on the other hand, are more subtle, and are more often a product of verbal interactions between characters. Third, pro-social behaviours are frequently performed by female, non-white characters which introduces an extra variable that might conceivably influence the likelihood of their being imitated by the children who view them.

A second focus of interest in the pro-social effects of the media has been in the possible ways in which the media might influence the moral reasoning of people who watch it. Critics have suggested that television is capable only of corrupting the morality of viewers (e.g. by showing people bending or breaking moral codes), but critics argue that this is not the case. Those who defend the value of the media with respect to morality argue that television can present and engage with moral issues in an entertaining and stimulating way. Ryan (1976) believes that television can act as moral teacher and counsellor through its portrayal of difficult moral issues in soap operas and television talk shows. Despite these claims, however, there is little evidence to support the claims for television's role in this respect.

One study carried out by Rosenketter et al. (1990) asked parents to keep a television diary of the viewing habits of their children over a two-week period. The researchers then investigated whether television viewing was in any way linked to the moral reasoning capabilities of the children involved. Among four- to five-year-old children, heavy television viewing (regardless of type) was linked to less advanced moral reasoning. This did not show that watching certain types of television impaired the moral development of the children (in contrast to the critical views stated earlier). Among seven- to eight-year-olds, there was a strong preference for watching situation comedies which involved families. The seven- to eight-year-olds in the study did show enhanced understanding of helping others who were in need. This was the theme of most of these types of shows. The study also demonstrated that among the oldest children (aged ten to eleven) their preference for adult action-adventure shows was linked to a less well-developed awareness of the needs of others.

The evidence for the pro-social effects of television and other media is still not conclusive, but it is clear that under certain situations, pro-social television can counteract the potentially harmful effects of the anti-social content of the same media.

Section B

5. Discuss the effects of predator–prey and symbiotic relationships on the evolution of behaviour patterns. **(24 marks)**

> **TIP**
>
> This rather clumsy-sounding question is taken almost word-for-word from the AEB syllabus and, as that's where the questions come from, you should be prepared for questions like this. This question is asking you to describe and evaluate the effects of (remember, that's what 'discuss' means) *both* predator–prey *and* symbiotic relationships. When you get questions that ask you to do more than one thing (as here), and you only discuss one of these (lets say, predator–prey relationships) you are showing 'partial performance' and will only receive partial marks. It isn't a straightforward halving of the marks as you might expect, but a maximum of 8 out of 12 marks for each of the skills (A and B).

Predators have developed a great variety of different strategies for catching and killing their prey. Prey have also responded to these strategies over evolutionary time by developing equally effective anti-predator behaviours. This predator–prey relationship, where the development of characteristics in one is reflected by corresponding developments in the other, is known as the biological arms race. For example, many of the special characteristics of prey species have evolved purely as a result of the pressure that predators exert on them. An example of this is the development of bat detectors in mice: if bats did not exist, then mice would not have developed bat detectors. Many other characteristics in prey species such as speed and group vigilance during feeding, are seen as a direct result of the pressures exerted by predators.

Among the strategies used by predators are stalking, ambushing and communal hunting. Some snake species, such as the cobra, will actively stalk their prey, whereas others, such as the rattlesnake, tend to lie in wait for their victims. Other species, such as wolves, will hunt in packs. This has the advantage of letting these animals catch more prey, and deal with large prey that would be too difficult to deal with otherwise. Killer whales, for example, are more able to catch much larger whales through cooperation in their hunting.

Research by Curio (1976) on the effectiveness of different predator strategies has failed to provide any significant insights other than that the success rate of predators is rarely high, whatever the strategy used. Most of the time the strategies that prey have developed in response to the pressure of their predators enables them to escape.

Prey have also developed highly successful strategies to avoid being eaten by predators. The use of unpredictable movements (known as protean displays), such as zigzagging and jumping, makes it difficult for predators to follow. Other prey species have evolved characteristics as mimics so that they appear to possess the characteristics of animals that are dangerous to the predator. For example, the hawkmoth caterpillar has evolved snake-like characteristics. If disturbed, the caterpillar detaches its posterior end from the branch and moves it in a snake-like manner.

The term 'symbiosis' refers to any evolutionary development where one species has, over evolutionary time, adapted to the presence of the other. Harré and Lamb (1986) identify three kinds of symbiotic relationship. These are commensalism, where one partner benefits and the other is not affected; parasitism, where one party benefits and the other loses out; and mutualism, where both parties benefit. Although it is difficult to prove that in a commensalist relationship one partner remains unaffected, there are a number of species where this arrangement is evident. The cattle egret feeds on insects that are disturbed by large mammals. Scavenger millipedes live in the nests of ants where they gain some protection and gain from the scavenging forays of the ants.

True symbiosis is often represented in terms of mutualistic relationships. An example of this kind of mutualistic relationship is the sea anemone and the clown fish. The fish gain protection from predators by hiding in the stinging tentacles, but because of a protective slime covering their bodies, they are not stung themselves. The sea anemone gains from this relationship in that it gets food scraps that the fish takes into its tentacles to eat. Other kinds of mutualistic relationship involve cleaning relationships such as the one found between cleaner fish and larger predatory fish living on the reef. Cleaner fish such as the cleaner wrasse approach the host fish by using a specially evolved display. This inhibits the host fish from attacking the cleaner which then removes the parasites from its skin and even inside its mouth.

As mentioned earlier, the relationship between predator and prey is a product of the biological arms race. The significance of this arms race is that each member of the predator–prey relationship contributes to the selective pressure of the other. This means that evolution is a process of measure and counter-measure with neither ever developing significant advantages over the other. Dawkins (1976) suggests that although neither predator nor prey ever develop a significant advantage, it is usually the prey that are more successful. He gives two main reasons for this. The first is the idea of an 'evolutionary budget'. Predators normally evolve strategies to catch a number of different prey, and are therefore not specialists at catching any one prey species. Prey, on the other hand, 'invest' more of their evolutionary 'budget' in developing characteristics and strategies that enable them to evade a small number (or in some cases only one) of predator species. This makes them more specialised in their part of the predator–prey relationship, and therefore more successful. The second reason is the 'life–dinner' principle, where prey are escaping for their lives, and predators are only seeking a meal. Failure for the prey will mean death whereas failure for the predator will only mean not eating that particular time. Prey are therefore more highly motivated to avoid capture than are predators to catch them.

The effects of predation may also benefit the prey species. Predators take as a large proportion of their prey the sick and the lame (as opposed to healthy animals). By taking the sick they help prevent the spread of disease and parasites, and by taking the lame and deformed they prevent weaker animals from breeding. Although this is a consequence of such actions, it is simply in the interests of predators to chase prey that will not put up much of a fight (thus conserving predator energy and safety).

The development of symbiotic relationships in animals enables animals to gain as a result of the presence of another animal. For example, in the cleaner fish described earlier, the removal of parasites is vital to the good health of the host. In situations where the cleaners are removed from a section of the reef, the hosts eventually become overrun by parasites and this increases both the frequency of disease and mortality rates. The origins of this type of relationship are not clear, but it seems likely that they first appeared as a form of parasitism where one animal 'invaded' the habitat of another. Through the process of natural selection, the 'invaded' animal developed 'counter-measures' which enabled it to take advantage of the parasite's presence. Other types of symbiotic relationship demonstrate a carefully weighed process of costs and benefits. For example, small birds sometimes nest under the edge of larger birds such as eagles. This gives the birds some protection from other predators, and the benefits this gives them outweighs the possible risk of predation from the eagles. Likewise, some animals have developed a symbiotic relationship with humans, and it is possible that some aspects of domestication can be attributed to the development of such symbiotic relationships.

6. Discuss the nature and consequences of sexual selection in evolution. (24 marks)

> **TIP**
>
> Sometimes questions take a little thinking about in order to tease out what is Skill A and what is Skill B (in AEB questions). In this case, the question setter has intended a description of the *nature* of sexual selection to be Skill A, and an evaluation of the *consequences* of sexual selection to be the Skill B content. This is important as there will be 12 marks for the former and 12 marks for the latter. This has implications not only for the way that the examiner apportions marks for the content you present, but also for the way that you apportion your time and effort when actually writing the answer. This question doesn't rule out sexual selection in humans, but that sort of content is often more speculative than psychologically informed, so be careful what you include.

Sexual selection relates to the selection within nature of characteristics which are solely concerned with increasing an animal's mating success. It works by favouring the development of traits in one sex (usually males) that enable animals to compete directly against each other in order to gain access to, and matings with, the other sex. This process is known as intra-sexual selection, or mate competition. Sexual selection also favours the development of traits in one sex that enables animals to attract members of the other sex. This process, known as intersexual selection, is based on the understanding that in many species, reproductive success for one sex is determined by the choice of the other sex. Sexual selection, therefore, favours the development of traits that are attractive, for whatever reason, to members of the opposite sex.

Competition as a result of sexual selection is at its greatest when there is a large difference in the amount of parental investment between the sexes and where the ratio of males to females is imbalanced. As males typically invest less than females, particularly in species where fertilisation is internal, they are more likely to compete to obtain as many matings as possible.

In some species, males scramble to be the first to locate receptive females and will fight over them if more than one male locates a female at the same time. In some species of squirrel, individual animals are widely dispersed and have only a short breeding season. Males must range widely in their search for females and often several males locate an individual female at the same time. The males then engage in chases, and ultimately one male drives the other males away. The most successful male is not necessarily the most dominant, but the one that covers the most ground (Schwagmeyer, 1988). If females tend to be found in groups, a single male may attach himself to the group and defend it against other males, thus gaining exclusive access to the females in the group. This appears to be the basis of male inclusion in many mammalian groups.

When the oestrus periods of females are relatively synchronised, males may attempt to control the group only once during the mating season. This is supported by studies of Scottish red deer (Clutton-Brock et al., 1982). The rut lasts about a month, and dominant stags attempt to keep together as larger group of females as possible for as long as they can for that period. As well as keeping the females together and mating with them, the stags must also fight off other intruding stags. This constant defence during the rutting period is very expensive, with stags losing 20% of their weight during the rut. The risks of injury during this period are also considerable.

If female receptivity is less synchronised, a male may stay with a female group throughout the year. This is evident in a number of species, including lions and langurs. In both of these species, the new male will attempt to kill all the young unweaned animals in the group. These cubs have been fathered by the previous male, and therefore it does not benefit the new male to provide for them. A female cannot produce another cub whilst she is lactating, but after her cub is weaned she becomes ready to reproduce again; by killing the cubs, the males can bring forward the time when the female is ready to reproduce again. There are a number of counter-tactics that can be utilised by females. Some females leave the group until their infants are weaned. Pregnant females often show pseudoestrus, copulating repeatedly with the new male, and thus confusing paternity of the newborn later on. The one thing that females cannot evolve is a tendency to refuse to mate with infanticidal males, for to do so would limit their total lifetime number of offspring (Grier and Burk, 1992). Although infanticide has clear benefits for males, it is not a common occurrence in nature. This may be for a number of reasons. First, in some species, females are bigger than males and are therefore physically able to prevent it. Second, the advantage of infanticide depends on a high frequency of male takeover, and a long lactational delay of ovulation. When neither of these conditions are present, males gain less by being infanticidal.

A consequence of intense competition between males is that they are relatively unrefined in their choice of potential mate. Because males tend to invest very little in their own sperm, the costs of poor mating choice would consequently be low. Sperm is easily replaceable, although poor discrimination of mates might make a male more susceptible to predators (Burk, 1982). For females, on the other hand, the costs of making a poor choice of mate may be high. Mating with a member of another species, for example, results in a profound decrease in her lifetime fitness, because valuable eggs take time and energy to replace. Thus it is important to ensure that a male is of the right species. One consequence of this need is that individual species have evolved species-specific sexual signals. Once species-specific pairing has occurred through female response to sexual signals, no possibility of confusion can arise (Grier and Burk, 1992).

As well as choosing a male of the right species, females must select potential mates on the basis of important characteristics. These may include choosing a compatible genotype where an optimal degree of inbreeding is favoured. If different variants of a species lived in slightly different habitats, and have adapted to those habitats, hybrid offspring would be less well-adapted. If females chose mates that were genetically too similar, however, they would increase the risk of producing offspring with rare, harmful combinations of recessive alleles. One of the puzzling questions concerning sexual selection is how does it explain the development of spectacular ornamentation in males? It is obvious why a male who possesses a good territory or who provides prenuptial gifts would be attractive to a female, but not males who simply possess bright plumage or a longer tail.

One of the first explanations for this type of preference came from Fisher (1930). Fisher proposed that the trait being chosen was an indicator of the male's 'true vigour'. A male bird that possessed a long tail may also have possessed increased fitness (perhaps through enhanced foraging ability). If a gene arose whereby females were more likely to mate with long-tailed males, then females would be able to increase their own fitness by choosing these males. Tails would thus lengthen to a point where they had negative consequences (e.g. decreased adaptive viability). Females could not escape from this runaway process, because females who mated with short-tailed males would have short-tailed sons and probably no grandprogeny.

One possible explanation of how such a preference might have started in the first place has been proposed by Hamilton and Zuk (1982). Males would be chosen for their bright plumage or ability to sustain prolonged courtship displays because this is an indication of vigour and resistance to disease. An alternative explanation from Trivers (1985) proposes that females may choose among males on the basis of traits that are relatively unimportant for their sons, but important to their daughters. An example of such a trait would be the expensive antlers of red deer stags. Although males incur costs in growing such structures, females who inherit such traits without actually producing them can put that capacity towards increased investment in their eggs or their young.

7. **'Why do animals live in groups?'**
Critically consider the role of sociality in non-human animals. (24 marks)

> **TIP**
>
> This question contains a quotation, although in this case there is no need to address it explicitly. The quotation is simply used to give a clue to candidates what we mean by the term 'sociality' (i.e. living in groups). The injunction used in this question is particularly significant. It requires not only a Skill A and a Skill B response, but also a particular type of Skill B response. In this question, you are required to present both the strengths and limitations (here translated as the advantages and disadvantages) of sociality. If you present only the advantages or the disadvantages you will be displaying the dreaded partial performance and will therefore lose marks.

Non-human animals form social links with other animals for a variety of reasons. Some raise their offspring as part of a breeding pair, and remain isolated from conspecifics, while other species exist in social groups where cooperation among conspecifics may be the norm. Some animals come together only for specific reasons such as mating or hunting, yet at other times are more solitary. Different groupings of animals depend very much on the functions of the behaviours being observed.

To some extent, all animals have some form of social organisation, even if it is only that necessary for sexual reproduction. Examples can be found in the defensive schooling of fish. The primary function of schooling is as an anti-predator defence, and as evidence for this, most schooling species are relatively small, and few predatory fish school. Schooling protects fish from predators in a number of ways. First, predators are less likely to encounter fish of a prey species if they stay clumped than if they disperse randomly (Partridge, 1981). The evolutionary response of predatory fish such as tuna and barracuda is to form loose hunting schools of their own. In this way, each individual benefits from the detection of a school, as each predator would notice if his neighbour found food.

In addition to the anti-predator functions of schooling, shoals serve a number of social functions. They may bring members of different sexes together for breeding or may allow individuals to copy each other. It is now established that fish in groups learn more quickly than when they are alone, but it is not known whether this is due to increased attention as a result of being with others, or to imitation. It has also been suggested that schooling has important functions during migration, where the presence of many individuals may result in a more accurate determination of orientation (Partridge, 1981). If individual estimates of the correct direction for migration were normally distributed, then the consensus of the group would be more accurate than any one individual.

Another suggestion about why fish school is that they might confuse a predator who is confronted by a large number of prey simultaneously. This confusion effect may operate at two levels. First, it may operate in the brain of the predator, who may not be able to make up his mind which fish to attack. Second, it may operate at the periphery, with movement from one fish distracting the predator from being able to catch another. Much of the confusion effect appears to be caused by the identical appearance of the prey. Predators seem to prefer individuals that look different in some way, or who behave differently to the rest.

Some species establish dominance relationships whereby some individuals acquire a high status, usually as a result of aggression, whilst others retain a low status. In stable groups, individuals come to recognise each other, and a dominance hierarchy is formed. Dominant individuals are able to use their status to gain priority to resources such as food, mates and nesting places. Dominance relationships are normally established by means of aggressive encounters. Once a dominance–subordinance relationship is established between two individuals, the aggressive encounter does not have to be repeated on future occasions. Instead, the relationship is maintained by means of agonistic displays, with the dominant animal asserting his dominance by means of threat displays. Subordinate animals are normally able to stay in the vicinity of dominant animals by employing appeasement postures. This enables them to share the advantages of group living (e.g. protection from predators and access to resources) without being attacked by the dominant animal.

Grier and Burk (1992) suggest a number of benefits of sociality. The first of these is the foraging advantages that may be obtained through group living. If food is unpredictably located, animals can obtain information about the location of feeding sites from conspecifics. In some species this may be more exploitive rather than communicative, but in others there is an active transmission of information between (usually related) individuals. For other social foragers, the problem may not be finding food, but catching it. Research evidence has shown that as the number of hunters increase, so does the success of the hunt. Such increased success may be achieved at the cost of sharing the food with co-hunters, however. Research by Kruuk, (1972) showed that when hunting wildebeest calves, single hyenas tended to be successful in only 15% of cases, whereas they were successful in 74% of cases when hunting in pairs.

A second advantage of group living is in the reduced risks of predation compared with solitary animals. Because of the greater number of 'eyes' in a group of animals, predators are more likely to be spotted at a greater distance and are therefore less likely to make a successful attack. Kenward (1978) released a trained goshawk and observed its hunting success with flocks of pigeons. The success rates of the goshawk declined from 80% for solitary pigeons, to less than 10% against flocks of more than 50 pigeons. A related advantage is the production of alarm calls so that when one individual spots a predator, all members of the group are immediately informed. As the immediate beneficiaries of this apparently altruistic behaviour are likely to be genetic relatives, this has an advantage even for the calling animal who may be taken by the predator. An added advantage of living in larger flocks is that the percentage of time spent being vigilant is less, thus releasing time to be spent on other activities.

The most obvious disadvantage of group living is that it automatically increases competition for access to food, mates and living conditions. The costs of this competition may be a decrease in the amount of food consumed by individuals within the group, and as a consequence, a decrease in the number of eggs produced by females within the group (Reichert, 1985). This increased competition also leads to aggressive behaviour, which is demanding in terms of energy, increases the risk of serious injury, and may distract attention away from potential predators. Evidence from Hoogland (1979) demonstrated that among prairie dogs, larger colonies had several times as many aggressive interactions per individual per hour than in smaller colonies.

A second cost of group living is the increased rates of parasitism and disease. When animals are closely packed together, there is a much greater opportunity for the transmission of parasites and pathogens. This may be through direct contact between group members, or indirectly through contact with nests, soil, sand and so on. Evidence from Hoogland (1979) found that among prairie dogs, the major parasites are rodent fleas, many of which carry the bubonic plague bacterium. Plague epidemics are reasonably frequent events among prairie dogs, and the resulting levels of mortality tend to be higher than can be replaced by annual reproduction.

8. Describe and evaluate one or more explanations of foraging behaviour. (24 marks)

> **TIP**
>
> This question has used the instruction 'one or more'. It is usual in AEB questions for them to state how many theories or explanations are required. Thus, you could be asked to describe and evaluate *two* explanations of foraging behaviour, but as there is one major explanation (optimal foraging theory), the question has recognised that. You could either concentrate on the one theory or choose more than one. The choice is entirely yours. One thing you should be wary of, however, is the temptation to present far too many explanations so that your answer is little more than a superficial gloss over. Questions in comparative psychology rarely attract much evaluation, but they can be evaluated in much the same way as any other type of question. One effective way of doing this is through looking at research that supports or contradicts the main claims of a theory.

The major theory that explains the foraging behaviour of animals is *optimal foraging theory* (OFT). This theory looks at feeding from a benefit/cost standpoint. It states that animals should feed or change their feeding behaviour in a manner that maximises the benefits and minimises the costs. The ultimate measure of the benefits of any feeding strategy is increased fitness (i.e. the reproductive output of an animal and its descendants) but this is difficult to assess in the short term. The more usual way of assessing benefits is through calculation of the calories ingested during foraging minus the calories expended.

Specifically, OFT proposes that animals should forage in such a way as to maximise their rate of calorific intake related to the time spent foraging. The time spent foraging can be divided into two parts, search time (time spent locating food) and handling time (time spent catching, killing, manipulating and ingesting food) When food is available in limited supply efficient foragers that have maximised this relationship would have an advantage over those that have not. Even if food is not limited, OFT proposes that efficient foragers are favoured because this releases time for other important behaviours. Additionally, as foraging exposes the forager to predators, efficient foraging may minimise that vulnerable period.

The type of food an animal chooses may be governed by OFT. Animals can be classed on a continuum from generalists which eat almost anything they can ingest, to others that engage in specialised foraging. Some species are so highly specialised that they feed only on particular parts of a plant or animal. Generalists have more types of food available to them but they may be less efficient at catching any one specific type of prey. OFT would predict that generalists usually have shorter search times for finding prey but longer handling times than would a specialist for that type of prey. Laverty (1988) demonstrated this with specialist-feeding bumblebees who found the nectar more efficiently when presented with their speciality plant compared with other generalist species of bee.

OFT also predicts that animals should choose the most profitable food items among those available and ignore unprofitable food outside the optimal range no matter how common it is. In food-rich environments a narrower range of foods would be taken and in food poor environments the diet should be broader. These OFT predictions have been supported in numerous cases; for example, pinon jays assess the quality of pinon seeds and take only the good ones (Ligon and Martin, 1974). In a study of crows feeding on whelks (Zach, 1979) crows chose larger whelks because these were more likely to break when dropped from height. Smaller whelks were ignored despite the fact they were more common and easier to carry. The energy gain from the more efficient use of large whelks gave a net advantage as predicted by OFT.

In animals that catch their prey, there may be several potential prey of the same species available at the same time. Potential prey may vary in their ease of capture or their ability to fight back. In such cases it is advantageous for the predator to discriminate between those that are worth the effort and those that are not. One common assumption is that predators take only the sick and unfit (referred to as the BBC theorem by Dawkins (1982) because it appears so often in natural history documentaries). This, it is claimed, preserves the quality of the prey and maintains the balance of nature. It is unlikely that the predators are acting in the interests of the prey, but their interests in not wasting effort or avoiding injury would appear to have the same effect.

Apart from the time spent, the cost of a foraging activity may also be determined by the energy expenditure during foraging. Theoretically it may be advantageous for a forager to use one method rather than another under different circumstances. In economic terms, there is a break-even point where the forager expends more energy than it is taking in. In such circumstances it may profit the forager to switch to a cheaper (in terms of energy expenditure) method although the intake is lower. Under these circumstances the net benefit may be higher than with the expensive method. Grubb (1977) found that ospreys have a number of methods of searching for prey, but hovering leads to the most successful number of catches. It is also the most expensive in terms of energy, and in poor visibility ospreys switch to one of the cheaper methods.

Critics of OFT have argued that the theory amounts to circular reasoning, i.e. an animal is foraging optimally if its behaviour fits the predictions of the theory. There may be many other reasons why an animal's behaviour might or might not fit the optimality model. First, animals may not be seen to forage optimally because high calorie foods lack other important nutrients. An animal may have to eat a variety of foods to ensure a balance of nutrients. Second, foragers may appear to be less than optimal to an observer who has a false idea of what an animal's behaviour has actually been selected to do. Pyke (1979) found that golden-winged sunbirds did not appear to forage optimally in terms of energy intake, but did behave as predicted in terms of minimising the costs of foraging.

A further problem in assessing optimality is the fact that animals do not reproduce as a result of foraging alone. Optimal foraging may be sacrificed so that a more generally optimal balance of different behaviours is achieved. The other behaviours might include territorial defence and watchfulness for predators. Milinski (1978) discovered that sticklebacks feed in lower density areas of daphnia when they have to watch for kingfishers. An important drawback of OFT models is that they only consider the individual forager and its food rather than the presence of other competing foragers. A particular influence on the efficiency of an animal's foraging behaviour is its social status. Dominant animals may be able to forage optimally whereas subordinate animals frequently keep an eye open both for predators and harassing dominants and therefore appear to forage non-optimally.

Module Paper 5 marking scheme

Section A

1. Discuss research into the effects of any two drugs on behaviour. **(24 marks)**

> **TIP**
>
> As mentioned in the previous marking scheme, there is a tendency for AEB questions to prescribe how many of a particular thing are required. In this question, there is an instruction to discuss research into the effects of *two* drugs. These might be clinical drugs or 'recreational' drugs. The clinical drugs are easier to write about because research on the so-called recreational drugs is harder to come by, and students often resort to anecdotes and speculation in lieu of actual research evidence. You are required to discuss *two* drugs, so if you ignore that instruction and write about more than two, only the best two will be marked. It is also worth pointing out that the word 'behaviour' includes changes at a neurophysiological level, and thus should make answering this type of question a lot easier. Don't worry too much about the spelling of complicated drugs – it is quite acceptable to have a stab at it and get it slightly wrong.

This essay will discuss research relating to two classes of drug, the anti-psychotic drugs which are used to alleviate the symptoms of the psychoses, and anti-anxiety drugs which are used to reduce anxiety. The first anti-psychotic to have a significant effect on the treatment of schizophrenics was chlorpromazine, which, in common with other anti-psychotic drugs such as haloperidol and thioridazine, acted as dopamine antagonists. This meant that these drugs blocked synaptic receptors for the neuro-transmitter dopamine, and thus reduced dopamine transmission in the brain. This led to the conclusion that if effective drugs blocked dopamine synapses, then schizophrenia must be due to dopamine overactivity in the brain (Green, 1996). Evidence from Seeman et al. (1976) showed that the more effective a drug is at blocking dopamine receptors, the more effective it is for relieving schizophrenia. Exposure to high levels of chlorpromazine produced a specific alleviation of agitated schizophrenic patients, but catatonic or emotionally blunt schizophrenics were activated.

An important feature of the anti-psychotic effects of chlorpromazine is that it is frequently associated with motor effects similar to those found in sufferers of Parkinson's disease. At the same time that the drug begins to have an effect on the schizophrenic symptoms, it often begins to elicit mild tremors, muscular rigidity and a general decrease in voluntary movement (Pinel, 1993). More recent anti-psychotics such as clozapine are often referred to as 'atypical' anti-psychotics because they have different pharmological actions in the brain compared with established anti-psychotics such as chlorpromazine. Clozapine does not produce Parkinsonian side-effects, nor does it induce tardive dyskinesia, a motor disorder that develops in some patients who have been maintained on chlorpromazine for a number of years. However, because clozapine may, in some cases, produce a dangerous reduction in white blood cells and therefore the body's immune system, it is only prescribed for patients who have not responded to traditional anti-psychotics such as chlorpromazine, and whose white blood cell count remains at normal levels throughout therapy. There is growing evidence (Kerwin, 1994) that newer anti-psychotics such as clozapine can improve negative symptoms in some patients, although the basis of this effect is still to be established.

Harrison (1995) points out that only about a third of schizophrenics respond well to anti-psychotic drugs, with another third responding partially. Research studies have shown that those patients who have shown improvement under drug therapy are likely to relapse if they stop taking them. This demonstrates that although anti-psychotic drugs do not *cure* schizophrenia, they do suppress the symptoms of the disorder through their pharmacological effect on the brain, thus allowing people with the disorder to lead close to normal lives because of the drugs they are taking. An added problem is that the results of research that has investigated the suppressant effects of chlorpromazine on dopamine synapses are equally compatible with an alternative explanation, the glutamate hypothesis of schizophrenia. According to this view, the underlying problem is deficient activity in glutamate synapses. The drug phencyclidine (angel dust) which inhibits glutamate receptors, produces symptoms that mimic schizophrenia even more closely than do the dopamine stimulants.

Drug therapy in the treatment of anxiety has concentrated almost exclusively on generalised anxiety disorder, and on one particular class of drugs, the benzodiazepines (BZs). BZs are both anxiolytic (anxiety reducing) and sedative (sleep inducing) so they are valuable in both anxiety disorders and insomnia. BZ drugs such as librium, valium and mogadon have become the most prescribed drugs in the history of psychiatry (Green, 1996). Although most psychoactive drugs act on neurotransmitter systems such as dopamine and serotonin, BZs act on specific BZ receptors found in synapses in the brain. This suggests that there must be a natural BZ-like neurotransmitter in the brain whose normal function is to stimulate the BZ receptor. Because of the sedative effects of the BZs, it seems likely that the BZ-like chemical that is presumably secreted by some neurons in the brain plays a role in the control of sleep.

These drugs exert their effects through the $GABA_A$ receptor. These sites contain binding sites for at least three different transmitter substances and neuromodulators, including the neurotransmitter GABA, barbiturates, alcohol and BZs. Because GABA is an inhibitory neurotransmitter, whenever these binding sites are activated the net effect of the barbiturates, alcohol and the BZs is to increase neural inhibition. The anti-anxiety effect of BZs depends on how the drug affects the amygdala, and to a smaller extent, the hypothalamus. Research by Sanders and Shekhar (1995) found that a small amount of BZ injected directly into a rat's amygdala decreased avoidance behaviour and increased social interactions with an unfamiliar partner. This suggests that ordinarily a rat is slow to approach an unfamiliar partner because of anxiety of how the other will react. A decrease in anxiety, therefore, leads to an increase in socialisation.

Although BZs are safer than barbiturates, which produce tolerance, withdrawal symptoms and convulsions, they are not without their adverse side effects. They often result in daytime lethargy, and are addictive. As insomnia is one of the after-effects of BZ exposure, they can actually exacerbate the very problem they were designed to correct (Pinel, 1993). When used over short periods of time, BZs do not lead to dependency or a withdrawal syndrome. However, they tend to be prescribed over much longer periods and under these circumstances, they do produce physical dependency and withdrawal symptoms in a significant number of patients (Green, 1996). The severity of withdrawal symptoms may prevent patients attempting to come off these drugs, and the sheer number of people using BZs means that the dependency problem is substantial (Green, 1996). BZ takers may also experience psychological dependence where dependence is more due to a drive to continue taking the drug because of the way that it makes us feel.

BZs are effective for short periods of extreme anxiety or insomnia, but beyond that they do not have any significant clinical action. As they also have side-effects, such as memory problems, confusion and loss of coordination, and adverse withdrawal reactions, their use remains controversial. Anxiety is thought to result from a decrease in GABA activity, and it is this effect that BZs attempt to correct. The biggest challenge to this theory comes from the introduction of a new drug, buspirone, into clinical practice. Buspirone is not a BZ, it does not bind to GABA receptors, yet it is just as effective in the treatment of anxiety as the BZs. In addition, it does not produce sedation or withdrawal effects.

2. **Describe and evaluate two methods used to investigate cortical functioning.** (24 marks)

> **TIP**
>
> This is a good question with which to practise your 'eight paragraph rule' for writing essays (see 'How to use this book'). This is a question that has four distinct parts. The first is a description of one method used in the investigation of cortical functioning, the second an evaluation of that method, the third a description of the second method, and the fourth an evaluation of that method. Given that you have eight paragraphs in total, that makes two paragraphs (between 200 and 250 words) for each of these parts. It is relatively easy to think of 100 words at a time, and project those words mentally onto the page in front of you.
> Make sure that the methods you are describing have actually been used in the investigation of *cortical* functioning rather than some other aspect of brain functioning.

Electrical stimulation of the brain (ESB) involves the application of a weak electrical current to a specific area of the brain. By adjusting the current, a 'false' nerve impulse is produced which 'fools' the brain into thinking that it has received an impulse from one of its sensory receptors. Electrical stimulation of a particular brain structure usually has behavioural effects that are the opposite of those produced when the same area is lesioned. Stimulation in the visual cortex may produce the sensation of flashes of light, and likewise, stimulation within the auditory cortex may produce a buzzing sensation. Early studies using this technique enabled physiologists to draw a 'map' of the human cortex, relating specific areas of the cortex to specific muscle activity.

As well as being able to mimic the brain's activity, it is also possible to record it. By using single electrodes it is possible to record the activity of a single neuron (single-unit recording). Likewise, it is possible to record the activity of much larger clusters of neurons through the use of larger electrodes and the measurement of evoked potentials (multiple-unit recording). Because of the continuous activity in the brain it is difficult for the response to a single stimulus to stand out against the background 'noise'. A computer is thus used to analyse the responses produced by a series of stimuli and the evoked potential thus emerges. This process can thus be used to identify areas of the brain involved in different sensory processes.

ESB has provided us with invaluable information about how the brain works and, it is claimed, has also been valuable in treating a variety of different conditions (McIlveen and Gross, 1996). Electrical stimulation has been shown to have useful applications in the reduction of pain, where stimulation of particular locations within the brain can cause analgesia. This can be strong enough to serve as anaesthetic for surgery in rats (Reynolds, 1969). The same technique has been used in reducing chronic pain in humans. Fine wires are surgically implanted in the central nervous system and attached to a radio controlled transmitting device that enables the patient to administer electrical stimulation when necessary (Kumar et al., 1990).

ESB has enabled investigators to reach important conclusions about the connections between various parts of the brain and the involvement of any one area of the brain in particular behaviours. Valenstein (1977), however, is more cautious about these conclusions. First, he claims, no single area of the brain is likely to be the sole source of a behaviour or emotion. Second, behaviour produced as a result of ESB does not perfectly mimic natural behaviour, being more compulsive and stereo-typical. Third, the effects of ESB may be different at different times, with subjects tending to experience different emotions or produce different behaviours in response to the same stimulation at different times. Valenstein suggests that the belief that the brain is organised into neat compartments that can be discovered by ESB is simply a myth.

Another technique for investigating the living human brain is Positron Emission Tomography (PET). PET scans provide information about the metabolic activity of the brain. First, the patient receives an injection of radioactive 2-deoxyglucose (2-DG). Because of its similarity to glucose, 2-DG is taken up rapidly by the neurons in the brain, but unlike glucose, it cannot be metabolised and therefore accumulates in the active neurons until it is broken down and released. As the radioactive molecules of 2-DG decay, they emit subatomic particles called positrons which are detected by the scanner. A computer then determines which areas of the brain have taken up the radioactive substance, and it produces a picture of a slice of the brain, showing the activity level of various regions within that slice. Thus, if a PET scan is taken whilst a patient is reading, the scan will indicate the areas of the brain that are most active during that activity.

PET scans have been useful in diagnosing abnormalities in the brain (such as tumours), and can give surgeons vital information prior to surgery. PET scans have also been used to investigate possible differences in the brain activity of people with and without a particular psychological disorder. Research using PET scans have revealed that the pattern of neural activity in the brains of schizophrenics is different to that of non-schizophrenics. This has led investigators to the conclusion that the disorder must have a physical cause. Research has also shown that men have a more active brain metabolism than women in those areas of the brain concerned with sex and violence (Gur et al., 1995), thus leading to the suggestion that there are important sex differences in these behaviours.

Newer versions of the PET scan, such as Single Positron Emission Tomography (SPET) are able to focus on very small areas of the brain and thus map the different areas of the brain that are either functioning or not functioning during an activity (McIlveen and Gross, 1996). The SPET measures the blood flow into different areas of the brain during mental activity. The subject is first injected with a small amount of radioactive iodine which makes the blood vessels mildly radioactive. As the subject lies within a ring of detectors, the radiation emitted by the iodine is turned into a pulse of light and then into an electronic signal. A computer is then able to build up a cross-section of the brain by analysing these signals.

SPET scans have already demonstrated that patients with Korsakoff's syndrome (a result of heavy and prolonged use of alcohol) are more likely to suffer a significant loss of functioning in the front areas of the brain. The ability to correlate activity in different brain areas with psychological functioning has made PET and SPET scans the most useful or current computer-based techniques. However, the technique is extremely expensive and time-consuming, and machines that can carry out such procedures are found only in the largest research hospitals.

3. **Describe and evaluate two theories of dreams.** (24 marks)

> **TIP**
>
> As with the previous question, this one is tailor-made for the 'eight paragraph rule' approach to essay writing. Read the notes on that question for an insight into how to approach this one. There is a danger when answering a question like this in an examination to try and slip in a prepared answer on sleep. Many students try this, and inevitably lose most if not all of the marks available. There are lots of theories that deal explicitly with dreams and those are being questioned here. When choosing your theories, you should choose those which you feel you could answer in the most balanced way. In other words, some theories lend themselves more to critical evaluation than others. This is particularly the case with theories that have been subjected to empirical investigation. Many people would pick the Freudian theory of dreams. That would be completely acceptable (in fact I have chosen Freud's theory for this answer), but it is quite a difficult theory to evaluate effectively.

Freud's theory of dream function states that dreams are a sort of psychic safety valve that allow people to harmlessly discharge otherwise unacceptable and unconscious wishes and urges. During waking hours, such impulses are excluded from consciousness because of their unacceptable nature, but the expression of these impulses through dreams relieves the psychic tensions created during the day and gratifies our unconscious desires. Freud argued that our unconscious desires are not gratified directly in dreams. The *manifest content* of the dream (the dream as reported by the dreamer) is a censored and symbolic version of the *latent content* (its actual meaning). Freud believed that the meaning of a dream must be 'disguised' through symbolic representation because it consisted of wishes and desires that would be disturbing if expressed directly.

Freud believed that dreams provide a valuable insight into the motives that guide a person's behaviour. He believed that dreams often reveal deeply hidden conflicts, though these require painstaking interpretation due to their disguised nature. The task of the dream therapist was to decode the manifest content of a dream into its latent content. Several of Freud's patients reported dreams in which their fathers were somehow harmed, much to the patients' grief and horror. Freud believed that such dreams represented unconscious anger or resentment towards the father. Such feelings are seen as originating from the Oedipus complex, the male's jealousy about his father's sexual relationship with his mother.

Attempts to discover whether the Oedipus complex was universal, and whether Freud's interpretation of such dreams was correct, have generally failed to confirm the universality of Oedipus complex dreams. In a study of young boys in the Trobriand culture of New Guinea, Malinowski (1927) found that they frequently reported dreams in which their maternal uncles were hurt, but never their fathers. One possible interpretation of this is that in the Trobriand culture, maternal uncles, not fathers, are the males who train and discipline boys. In Viennese culture, it was the fathers who both had a sexual relationship with the mother *and* acted as the source of discipline. Malinowski's study suggests that dreams *do* serve a form of wish fulfilment, but hostility in such cases is directed not at the sexual 'rival', but at the source of discipline.

It is possible that dreams do have some meaning and may reflect important conflicts and issues in a person' life. However, Freud's view that conflicts are always disguised has been criticised. Fisher and Greenberg (1977) argue that there is no rationale for approaching a dream as if were really a 'container for a buried secret wish', a person who is concerned with impotence is just as likely to dream about impotence as they are to dream about broken candles (symbolic transformation). McIlveen and Gross (1996) also suggest that the interpretation of a dream is not something that can be objectively achieved even if the interpreter is a trained psychoanalyst. As Collie (1993) argues, metaphors are notoriously ambiguous forms of communication, which are essentially just a system of images to be manipulated by the interpreter in any way they wish.

The 'activation synthesis theory' of dreaming (Hobson and McCarley, 1977) sees dreams as essentially random and meaningless. Research by Hobson (1989) showed that in cats certain cells in the brain fire in a seemingly random manner during REM sleep. The firing of these cells activates adjacent nerve cells, which are involved in the control of eye movements, balance and activities such as running and walking. Such body movements are inhibited during sleep but the signals are still sent to the parts of the cerebral cortex responsible for visual information processing and voluntary actions when we are awake. Although the body is not moving, the brain receives signals, which suggest that it is. In an attempt to make sense of this contradiction, the brain, drawing on memory, attempts to *synthesise* and make sense of the random bursts of neural activity.

The process of synthesis results in the brain imposing some order on the chaotic events caused by the firing of nerve cells, but it cannot do this in a particularly sophisticated way. This would explain why dreams often consist of shifting and fragmentary images. Hobson (1988) argues that *giant cells*, found in the reticular activating system are responsible for the onset of REM sleep. These cells are sensitive to the neurotransmitter acetylcholine. When this is available, the giant cells fire in an unrestrained way, but when there is no more of the neurotransmitter available, the cells stop. When acetylcholine becomes available again the giant cells start firing and another period of REM sleep begins.

The activation synthesis theory has attracted widespread support because of its explanatory power. For example, our tendency to dream about events that have occurred during the day presumably occurs because the most current neural activity of the cortex is that which reflects the concerns or events of the day (McIlveen and Gross, 1997). The activation synthesis theory is also capable of explaining why we do not experience smells and tastes during a dream. This is because the neurons responsible are not stimulated during REM sleep. Our inability to remember dreams is explained by the fact that the neurons that control the storage of new memories are 'turned off' during REM sleep. In a slightly different version of this theory, the brain is aroused and ready to process information during REM sleep. As the environment does not provide any, the sleeper processes information already existing in memory (Antrobus, 1986).

Foulkes (1985) criticises the activation synthesis theory because he claims that the content of dreams is influenced by our waking experiences and therefore dreams cannot be as random and psychologically meaningless as Hobson and McCarley suggest. The main criticism of the theory is that it does not suggest easily tested predictions, therefore it is difficult to validate its claims. The theory does not account for all the phenomena of dreams, or explain why many people have repetitive dreams or other dreams full of personal meaning (Winson, 1993).

4. (a) **Outline and evaluate one physiological theory of motivation.** (12 marks)

   (b) **Outline and evaluate one non-physiological theory of motivation.** (12 marks)

> **TIP**
>
> This is a very 'user-friendly' question, but one that would benefit from very careful reading. There are two distinct parts to the question, and the question setter has made no attempt to link the two parts in any way. Both have a Skill A and a Skill B component (outline and evaluate) but require quite different content. Each requires you to outline and evaluate *one* theory (more than one and only the best will be marked). The rather clumsy wording is an attempt to orient you towards one theory that is physiological in origin and one that is psychological. Unfortunately, asking for a psychological theory does not necessarily produce a non-physiological one because many people argue (perhaps rightly) that physiological theories are a part of the wider remit of psychophysiology.

(a) Drive reduction theory is normally associated with Hull (1943), who proposed that all behaviour was motivated, and that all motivation originates in the satisfaction of homeostatic drives such as thirst, hunger and temperature control. If, for example, an organism is deprived of food, this need state leads to an unpleasant state of arousal, experienced by the organism as a drive. These drive states initiate behaviour that is associated with their reduction. Once the organism has achieved whatever it needs (e.g. water, food or warmth), the behaviour ceases and the arousing drive state is reduced. The presence of an appropriate stimulus, therefore, reinforces the behaviours that led to its acquisition, and the organism thus learns as a result of that reinforcement.

Although the theory was originally formulated to explain the primary needs of hunger, thirst, etc., it has also been used to explain more complex human behaviour. Through association, we gradually learn secondary drives which are instrumental in some way in the reduction of primary drives. For example, if the mother provides nourishment (a primary reinforcer) for the infant, then by association with that food, she gradually acquires reinforcing qualities of her own. If the child is motivated to bring about the presence of the mother (a secondary reinforcer), the child is more likely to achieve the primary need of food. This explanation of the drive-reducing qualities of the mother was originally seen as the basis of the attachment band that forms between mother and infant.

There are a number of weaknesses with drive reduction theory. Hull's basic proposition was that organisms would not learn unless there were drives which could be reduced through reinforcement. Tolman (1948) showed how rats could learn mazes by developing cognitive maps, and without any reinforcement or drive reduction. It is now generally accepted that spatial learning is a highly developed ability in most animals and does not depend on drives or reinforcements (Olton, 1976). A second criticism arises from the proposal that when an organism reaches its goal, arousal is reduced and consequently the behaviour that led to that state is reduced. This is evidently not the case for all behaviours, unless there are an enormous number of drives, including curiosity, exploration and so on.

A final criticism of drive reduction theory comes from evidence from studies involving electrical self-stimulation of the brain. Olds and Milner (1954) discovered that if they implanted an electrode in certain parts of the brain (later identified as the median forebrain bundle) and allowed the rat to press a lever for self-stimulation, they would do so until exhausted. Hungry rats would ignore food and sexually receptive females in order to press the lever. Olds and Milner suggested that the median forebrain bundle acted as a pleasure centre in the rat brain, and that rather than reducing drive levels, reinforcement had the opposite effect and *increased* drive levels. Although similar findings have been found in a number of species, including humans, the explanation of human motivated behaviour in purely physiological terms is generally regarded as inadequate.

(b) Maslow (1954) proposed that human beings possess two sets of needs. The first set is concerned with basic survival, and includes physiological needs (such as the need for food, sex and sleep) and safety needs (such as the need for security and freedom from danger). Behaviours associated with these needs are seen as 'deficiency' motivated, as they are a means to an end. The second set of needs are more psychological needs and are associated with the realisation of an individual's full potential, and the need to 'self-actualise'. These needs are achieved more through intellectual and creative behaviours. Maslow's theory differs from more purely physiological representations of human motivation because motivation is seen as being not just concerned with tension reduction and survival, but also with human growth and development.

According to Maslow, human needs were arranged in the form of a hierarchy, with the survival needs at the bottom, and the more creative and intellectually oriented 'self-actualisation' needs at the top. Maslow argued that the survival needs must be satisfied before the individual can begin to satisfy the higher needs. The higher up the hierarchy, the more difficult it is to satisfy the needs associated with that stage, because of the interpersonal and environmental barriers that inevitably frustrate us. Higher needs become increasingly psychological and long term rather than being physiological and short term, as in the lower survival-related needs. Although Maslow did not believe that many of us could achieve true self-actualisation, he did believe that all of us experience transitory moments (known as 'peak experiences') of self-actualisation. Such moments, associated with personally significant events such as childbirth, sporting achievement and examination success), are difficult to achieve and maintain consistently.

Although critics of this theory might argue (and have argued) that the ordering of the needs is wrong (quoting the example of the artist who would rather paint than eat), this is a misrepresentation of the theory. Maslow would agree that lower needs must be 'relatively' satisfied before moving on to the next level, rather than completely satisfied. This does, however, challenge one of the central propositions of the theory, that needs are arranged in a hierarchical order. There is little direct empirical evidence for the theory. This is not surprising, as it is difficult to operationally define a concept such as self-actualisation, and therefore difficult to know how this might be tested experimentally. Maslow's own descriptions of self-actualised individuals were based on observations of individuals who he believed were self-actualised, rather than defining the term first and then testing whether certain individuals fitted its parameters.

A related criticism is that it is difficult to tell in Maslow's theory where the scientific leaves off and the inspirational begins. His theory is seen as more speculative than empirically proven, with a tendency to substitute rhetoric for research. Whilst it is true that Maslow's own work was rather informal and clinically descriptive, it did provide a rich source of ideas, and as such, a framework for discussing the richness and complexity of human motivation that goes beyond homeostatic models and other biological models (Green, 1996).

Section B

5. Describe and evaluate research relating to the causes and effects of any one emotional or behavioural problem in childhood (e.g. attention-deficit hyperactivity disorder or autism).

(24 marks)

> **TIP**
>
> This question is a nightmare to unravel when you are under examination conditions, but again it is fairly straightforward when you read it carefully. First, look at the subject content. The question requires any one emotional or behavioural problem in childhood. Examples are given, but these are not prescriptive. There are many other emotional and behavioural problems that could be used in this answer, but they should be problems of *childhood* rather than adulthood. If you use an unusual approach (childhood genius, for example), it is up to you to convince the examiner that this constitutes an emotional or behavioural problem. Note that the question does not ask for an emotional *and* a behavioural problem. Having chosen your problem, you now need to *describe* and *evaluate* research relating to the *causes* and *effects* of this problem. If we fit this to our 'eight paragraph rule', we get two paragraphs (approximately 200–250 words) describing research into the *causes* of the problem, two paragraphs evaluating this research, two paragraphs describing research into the *effects* of the problem, and two evaluating that research.

The symptoms of autistic disorder include a failure to develop normal social relations with other people, impaired development of communicative ability and lack of imaginative ability (Carlson, 1994). Bettleheim (1967) believed that the disorder developed in children whose parents were insufficiently emotional to form a bond with their child. As a result of failing to form this primary bond, it was believed that they would be unable to form a bond with anyone else. This explanation was soon discredited, however, as it was evident that parents of autistic children were just as caring and emotional as parents of children without the disorder. In the 1970s, Rutter saw autism as a form of language deficit as the disorder is always accompanied by a delay in the development of language. Although this theory suggested that autism was due to inborn abnormalities rather than deficiencies in parenting, Rutter himself disproved it when he found that children with specific language impairment made much better social adaptation than children with autism.

Frith et al. (1991) suggest that the impaired socialisation, communicative ability and imagination that characterise autism arise from abnormalities in the brain that prevent the child forming a 'theory of mind'. According to Frith, this means that the child is unable to predict and explain the behaviour of others in terms of their mental states (Frith, 1991). This explanation is supported by research carried out by Baron-Cohen et al. (1985) using the 'false belief test'. In this test, a child is told a story where an imaginary child (Mary) places something in one place and then goes outside. The object is then moved to a different place whilst Mary is elsewhere and unable to see the re-location. The child is then asked where they think Mary will look for the object. Children under the age of four typically answer that Mary will look in the new location despite the fact that she could not know that it has been moved. Children over the age of four are able to see things from another person's point of view, and appreciate that Mary could not have seen the switch. Children with autism typically fail theory of mind tests even when they are older than four.

A number of investigators have claimed that many of the problems experienced by children with autistic disorder can be attributed to a lack of theory of mind. But why do children with autistic disorder fail to develop a theory of mind? Leslie (1987) put forward a theory of pretend play that might explain why children with autistic disorder do not engage in pretend play and have a seeming inability to tell lies. Leslie suggests that before the age of about 18 months, normal children are unable to decouple their thoughts from reality. In other words, their view of the world is literal. Between the age of 18 months and 24 months, they develop a decoupler, a cognitive process that enables them to go beyond what they perceive and to think about alternative possibilities in their world. According to this model, the absence of this cognitive decoupler means that autistic children have difficulties about forming alternative ideas about the world.

One of the problems with this theory is that pretend play is present at two years, yet theory of mind does not develop until about four years of age (Messer and Messer, 1996). This can be explained in terms of the complexity of the theory of mind test, especially the need to make inferences about the beliefs of another. It may well be the case that children simply have trouble remembering all the components in the theory of mind tests, and this undermines their performance (Leslie, 1994). As Messer and Messer (1996) point out, it is important to return to the range of abilities of children with autism. In many studies, children with autism *are* able to pass the false belief test (sometimes as high as 50%). This finding is largely ignored, but it is important because it indicates that a theory of mind explanation may not be appropriate for all children with autism. An alternative cognitive explanation of autism suggests that children with autistic disorder experience 'stimulus over-selectivity', in that they tend to attend to only one dimension of a stimulus (Lovas et al., 1979). As a result of this, argues Lovas, autistic children have difficulty associating human beings with all the different things that they represent (security, warmth, gratification of needs), and therefore fail to develop a proper affection and a desire for social interactions.

Biological explanations of autism have become popular because the disorder tends to develop so early in life, before environmental factors have had much time to have an influence. Twin studies have shown that close genetic relatives of autistic children have an increased risk of developing the disorder, with identical twins having the highest risk of all (Rutter and Bartak, 1971). The genetic explanation has also received some support from the discovery of certain chromosomal abnormalities in about 10% of those with the disorder. Other research suggests that autism may be a consequence of neurological dysfunction, with autistic children having a higher number of neurological problems than other children (Gillberg et al., 1990). This view is supported by research that has found deficits in the left temporal lobe of autistic children. This is thought to be related to the linguistic and social impairments found in children with the disorder (White and Rosenbloom, 1992).

A final explanation of autism is that it is a consequence of unusual environmental stress. If events such as parental death, divorce or parental separation occur very early in life, this may traumatise the child, and as a result they may withdraw within themselves. As with other explanations that relate autism to environmental factors, support for this hypothesis is extremely thin, and no relationship has been found between stressful life events and autism (Cox et al., 1975). Some researchers have argued that autism may have multiple biological causes, and suggest that subgroups of the disorder might be identified according to the specific medical conditions associated with each case (Gillberg, 1992). There is a belief among researchers that all biological factors that are implicated in autism lead to a 'final common pathway' (Comer, 1992) that leads to an autistic behaviour pattern. As yet, there is disagreement about the location of this 'final common pathway' although suggestions include the reticular activating system, which arouses electrical activity in the cortex, abnormalities in the cortex itself, or neurotransmitter imbalances such as a high level of serotonin or dopamine activity.

6. (a) Describe either the DSM or ICD approach to the definition and classification of normal and abnormal behaviour. **(12 marks)**

　　(b) Evaluate this approach in terms of its practical problems and ethical implications. **(12 marks)**

> **TIP**
>
> If you have mastered the AEB Glossary of Terms, you will have noticed that the first part of this question is all Skill A and the second part is all Skill B. You are invited to write about *either* the DSM (Diagnostic and Statistical Manual) *or* ICD (International Classification of Diseases) approaches to the classification of normal and abnormal behaviour. Don't worry too much about the 'definition *and* classification' bit, as that is what they do anyway. Likewise, both of these classification systems deal with normal *and* abnormal behaviour, so you don't really have to worry about describing both aspects. At the time of writing, DSM-IV and ICD-10 are the current versions, but you don't have to be totally up to date with this. The second part of the question (a direct lift from the AEB syllabus, and therefore highly predictable) asks for an evaluation of *both* practical *and* ethical implications, so an examiner would be checking that you have included both of these.

The Diagnostic and Statistical Manual (DSM) is a classification, definition and description of over 200 mental health disorders. DSM is regularly updated, the most recent (1994) being DSM-IV. To avoid the potential difficulties which might be caused by the very different approaches to abnormal behaviour, DSM-IV emphasises the description of symptoms and the course of a disorder rather than the aetiology and treatment of disorders. Each of the mental disorders is conceptualised as a clinically significant behavioural or psychological syndrome that occurs in an individual and is associated with present distress or disability or with a significantly increased risk of suffering death, pain, disability or an important loss of freedom (DSM-IV, 1994). In addition, this syndrome must not merely be an expectable response to a particular event (e.g. death of a spouse).

In order to diagnose a problem, various procedures are used, including clinical interviews, observation of behaviour, medical records and psychometric tests. In order to classify a particular syndrome, DSM-IV uses a multiaxial system, that is a system of classification in which an axis groups disorders in terms of common features. The first two axes involve classification on the basis of symptoms, and the remainder relate to other factors that might be taken into consideration when making a diagnosis. As individuals may have multiple diagnoses across and within axes, full diagnosis involves taking all five axes into consideration. This constitutes a more holistic approach to the person and their mental health difficulty.

The first axis involves the clinical disorders. These are mental disorders which present symptoms or patterns of behaviour that are painful or impair an area of functioning. Examples would include schizophrenia and the anxiety disorders. The second axis includes personality disorders, which are dysfunctional ways of perceiving and responding to the world. Examples of personality disorders would be paranoid personality disorder and problems relating to abuse or neglect. The second axis of DSM-IV also includes disorders related to mental retardation. These are disorders that affect specific skills such as reading and language skills. The third axis refers to general medical conditions, which are physical problems that might be helpful in understanding, managing or treating a person's mental disorder.

Axes IV (psychosocial and environmental problems) and V (global assessment of functioning) provide important supplemental information about the social context of the disorder (e.g. relationships and environmental difficulties) and an assessment of the highest level of adaptive functioning during the previous year. Information about competence may help to predict the likely outcome of the disorder. For example, if a psychosocial stressor, such as a relationship problem, or a job loss, is identified and associated with the onset of depression, a positive outcome is more likely to be predicted. This is because the health difficulty is more likely to be a reaction to this stressor rather than being indicative of some internal cause. In this case, a return to the standard level of functioning is more rapid than if the cause of the stress were from within the individual concerned. The use of a classification system such as DSM-IV has a number of practical and ethical implications. The main purpose of such systems is to provide a universal definition and recognition of specific disorders. As such, DSM-IV provides a diagnostic shorthand for mental health professionals. With agreed terms and categories of disorders, effective communication concerning patients and their treatment is possible. An additional purpose of the DSM classification system is to assist clinicians to diagnose a person's problem as a particular disorder. Once diagnosed, the most appropriate course of treatment can be prescribed.

Davison and Neale (1994) suggest that classification systems should possess aetiological, concurrent and predictive validity. For classification systems to have aetiological validity there should be evidence that the same causal factors are evident for all individuals with a particular disorder. Because there is substantial disagreement about the aetiology of many disorders, this goal is difficult to meet. For a system to have concurrent validity, other symptoms that are not part of the disorder itself yet are characteristic of it, should be found in all those with that disorder. The classification categories of DSM-IV should also be able to predict the outcome of a disorder. Clinical research has established that certain treatments work most effectively with specific disorders (Zimbardo et al., 1995). Classification systems tend to suffer from a lack of reliability in that not all the same practitioners will arrive at the same diagnosis when presented with the same symptoms or information about a condition. The greater precision of the categories of DSM-IV has reduced this problem, although it is still evident, especially in certain disorders.

The term 'abnormal' is not used within the DSM classification as it serves no purpose in either diagnosis or treatment (Prentice, 1996). However, there still remains the tricky question of deciding whether a person is really showing the symptoms of a mental disorder or not. Scheff (1966) warns of the problem of 'nominalism'; that is, by attaching a label to distress or dysfunction of any kind, we may contribute to the construction of a new social role and thereby a new disorder. In turn, the prevalence of the 'disorder' thereby increases, partly by virtue of the increased recognition and categorisation, and partly by virtue of those who then come to act in accordance with the received meanings of that label (Zimbardo et al., 1995). The person who accepts the diagnosis and acts accordingly (e.g. by seeking 'help') is then reinforced, whereas the person who tries to escape from this diagnosis and its associated treatment is punished.

According to Prentice (1996), there is an inevitability about labelling. Absence from work, or from social functioning, requires an 'explanation', which usually entails labelling the problem. Those who suffer from mental disorders are usually confused and concerned about their condition. This can be extremely frightening, and therefore they are likely to seek help from a professional to help them label the problem. Such a label may then help to dispel what are often quite unwarranted fears about their condition. Many psychologists do not see the forcing of individuals into such tight diagnostic categories as desirable. It is seen as overlooking important individual differences between individuals. Many psychologists see the practice of labelling a set of symptoms within a classification system as unnecessary for effective psychological treatment.

7. Describe and evaluate social/psychological explanations of two anxiety disorders.

(24 marks)

> **TIP**
>
> You need to be careful here that you are actually writing about *anxiety disorders*. You would be amazed how many students start their essays on this topic with the words 'One type of anxiety disorder is depression (or schizophrenia, or anorexia or ...).'. The two most obvious examples of anxiety disorders are phobias and post-traumatic stress disorder. You could choose these two, or even two different phobias (but think, what different things could you say about them?). There are other anxiety disorders such as panic disorders and obsessive-compulsive disorders and these would be perfectly acceptable. Remember that this question asks for *two* disorders, not one or three. Social/psychological should indicate that you are giving non-biological explanations, the '/' meaning social and/or psychological. It is arguable whether genetic and neurophysiological explanations are truly 'psychological', but they would be acceptable here.

According to sociocultural theorists, *phobic disorders* are more likely to develop in people who are confronted with societal pressures and situations that pose real danger. Studies (e.g. Baum and Fleming, 1993) have shown that people in highly threatening environments are more likely to develop the general feelings of tension, anxiety, fatigue and sleep disturbances that characterise generalised anxiety disorders and the specific fears and avoidance behaviours that characterise phobic disorders. In the months after the Three Mile Island nuclear reactor accident, mothers of preschool children who lived in the vicinity were found to display five times as many anxiety or depressive disorders as mothers of comparable age and family structure living elsewhere (Baum, 1990). The Three Mile Island mothers still displayed elevated levels of anxiety a year after the accident.

One of the most direct indicators of societal stress is poverty. People without sufficient means typically live in homes that are more run down and communities with higher crime rates, have fewer educational and job opportunities and are at greater risk for health problems. Research indicates that poorer people have higher rates of phobic and generalised anxiety disorders. For example, research has shown that those who rely primarily on welfare or disability benefits for their income show a much greater prevalence of phobias than other people (Eaton et al., 1991). Although poverty and other societal pressures may establish a climate in which phobic and generalised anxiety disorders are more likely to develop, sociocultural variables are not the only factors at work. After all, most people in war torn, politically oppressed or endangered communities do not develop anxiety disorders. Theorists must still explain why some people develop these disorders and others do not.

Behaviourists believe that people with phobic and generalised anxiety disorders learn, through conditioning, first to fear and later to avoid certain objects, situations or events. Classical conditioning is a common way of acquiring fear reactions to objects that are not inherently dangerous. Two events that occur close together in time become closely associated so that the person then reacts similarly to both of them. Behaviourists agree that fears will undergo extinction if a person is repeatedly exposed to the feared object and sees that it brings no harm. After acquiring a fear response, however, most people try to avoid what they fear. Such avoidance behaviours develop through operant conditioning, the process by which we learn to behave in ways that are repeatedly rewarded. Avoidance effectively serves to reinforce avoidant behaviours and thus preserves their fear responses.

Studies have tended to support the claims of the behaviourists. Watson and Raynor (1920) taught a baby boy to fear white rats using classical conditioning procedures. According to some reports, Albert's fear of white rats also generalised to other objects such as rabbits, human hair and cotton wool. Research has also supported the behavioural position that fears can be acquired through modelling. Bandura and Rosenthal (1966) showed how subjects who observed a confederate apparently being shocked whenever a buzzer sounded, would themselves display a fear reaction whenever *they* heard the buzzer. Clinical case reports of anxiety disorders paint a similar picture. During World War II, cases were reported of combat airmen who became clinically anxious after observing other airmen display extreme anxiety (Grinker and Spiegel, 1945).

For some people, anxiety may persist well after a traumatic situation is over. Unlike other anxiety disorders, which are typically triggered by objects or situations that most people would not find threatening, situations that cause post-traumatic stress disorders (PTSD) would be traumatic for anyone. Recent studies have shown that childhood events seem to leave some people vulnerable to developing post-traumatic stress disorders in response to later traumatic experiences. People whose childhoods have been characterised by poverty, whose family members suffered mental disorders or who experienced assault or abuse at an early age, are more likely to develop PTSD in the face of later trauma than are people without such childhood experiences (Kolb, 1992).

It has been suggested that the tendency of many abused children to dissociate themselves from the experience and memory of abuse may become a habitual way of dealing with traumatic events in life. This leads them to wall off later traumas as well as setting the stage for the development of PTSD (Bremner, 1993). Other studies suggest that people with certain personality profiles are more likely to develop these disorders. It has been found, for example, that rape victims who had psychological problems before they were raped (Sales, 1984) and war veterans who had poor relationships before they went into combat (Chemtob, 1990) run a risk of developing prolonged stress reactions after traumatic experiences.

The idea that personality is related in some way to vulnerability to PTSD is further supported by research by Kobasa (1990) who discovered that many people respond to stress with a set of positive attitudes that she collectively referred to as *hardiness*. These help them to carry on their lives with a sense of fortitude, control and commitment. Those low in the traits of hardiness would show less ability to deal with traumatic events in such a constructive way. It has also been shown that people who are helped by strong social support systems (e.g. family and friends) after a traumatic event, are less likely to develop an extended disorder such as PTSD. In contrast, however, research has shown that weak social support networks have contributed to the development of PTSD in, for example, Vietnam war veterans (Figley and Leventman, 1990).

Although childhood experiences, personality and social support play important roles in a person's reactions to stress, the events that trigger PTSD can sometimes be so extreme and traumatic that they override a positive childhood, hardy personality and supportive social context. In a follow-up study of 253 Vietnam prisoners of war, it was discovered that five years after their release, 23% still required psychiatric help, despite the fact that all had been evaluated as well-adjusted before their imprisonment. It was found that it was those who had been imprisoned the longest and treated the most harshly that showed the highest percentage of anxiety related disorders (Ursano et al., 1981). Likewise, those who had witnessed the worst atrocities later experienced the most severe symptoms of PTSD (Yehuda et al., 1992).

8. (a) Describe one or more psychodynamic therapies. (12 marks)

   (b) Assess the appropriateness and effectiveness of this approach/these approaches for the treatment of psychological disorders. (12 marks)

> **TIP**
>
> Psychodynamic therapies help clients to uncover past traumatic events and the conflicts that have resulted from them. There are a number of dynamic therapies, but the one that most people have heard of is Freudian psychoanalysis. This question gives you the chance to write about more than one, but it isn't necessary. Do make sure you know the difference between a psychodynamic therapy and other forms of therapy (such as behavioural, humanistic, and so on). The second part of the question is asking you to assess the *appropriateness* and *effectiveness* of this therapy. Don't ignore the two different aspects of this assessment – they both have to be addressed. As should be obvious by now, 12 marks is half the total marks on offer for this question, so that means half the time.

Psychoanalysis is the name given to the therapy derived from the theory of Sigmund Freud. According to Freud, neurotic problems in later life are a product of the conflicts that arise during the Oedipal phase of development. These conflicts may be repressed because the immature ego is unable to deal with them at the time. The aims of psychoanalytic therapy are to create the right sort of conditions so that the patient is able to bring these conflicts into the conscious mind where they can be addressed and dealt with. Analysts use a variety of techniques to achieve these aims, including the following. In free association, the patient is encouraged to speak freely and to verbalise anything that comes to mind. In this way the patient may be able to bring content to the surface that has previously been censored by the ego.

Of particular significance during psychoanalysis are the patient's attempts at resistance. They may attempt to block discussion by changing the subject quickly, for example, or even neglecting to turn up for therapy. Freud considered these resistances a valuable insight into uncovering sensitive areas in the patient's unconscious mind. In dream analysis, the analyst attempts to unravel and interpret the symbolic nature of the patient's dreams. The true concerns of the patient are often disguised in their dreams and may be experienced symbolically, i.e. they dream about something that represents their concern, rather than dreaming directly about the concern itself. The true concerns of the patient are often disguised in this symbolic form to protect the conscious mind from developing full awareness of the underlying concern.

During analysis, the analyst offers interpretations of the patient's thoughts, actions and dreams, and points out their defences. By carefully waiting until the patient himself is about to gain the same insight the analyst can maximise the impact of the interpretation. Related to these interpretations is the problem of the patient's denial. The analyst may well have reason to believe that a patient's denial of an interpretation offered by the analyst is another example of the defensive process. Analysis of defences is emphasised by contemporary psychoanalysts (known as ego analysts) who dispute the relatively weak role that Freud assigned the ego (Davison and Neale, 1994). They argue that defence mechanisms are the ego's unconscious tools for warding off a confrontation with anxiety.

Of key importance in psychoanalytic therapy is transference. Freud had originally noticed that his patients sometimes felt and acted towards him as if he were an important person from the patient's past. Sometimes these feelings were positive, but sometimes they were negative and hostile. Freud assumed that these were relics of attitudes held toward these important persons in the patient's past. Freud felt that this transference was an inevitable aspect of psychoanalysis, and used it to explain to patients the childhood origins of many of the concerns and fears. In psychoanalysis, transference is seen as essential to a complete cure. Analysts use the fact that transference is developing as a sign that an important repressed conflict is nearing the surface.

Psychoanalytic therapy has been seen as appropriate mainly for the neurotic disorders (e.g. anxiety and eating disorders) rather than for the psychotic disorders such as schizophrenia. It is also used for depression although its effectiveness in this area is more questionable because of the apathetic nature of the depressive patients. A related problem is the greater likelihood of transference in depressive patients undergoing psychoanalysis. They are likely to show extreme dependency upon important people in their life (including their therapist) and therefore more likely to develop transference (Comer, 1995). Comer also suggests that psychoanalysis may not be appropriate for patients suffering from obsessive compulsive disorder in that it may inadvertently increase their tendency to over-interpret events in their life.

There has been criticism in recent years that if psychoanalysis is of benefit to people, it is only of benefit to those who possess certain qualities. The acronym YAVIS has been used to indicate that patients who are young, attractive, verbal, intelligent and successful would be the ones most likely to benefit from psychoanalysis. Few studies appear to support the first three of these suggestions, although as well as the latter two suggestions there is evidence that psychoanalysis also works best with those clients who are highly motivated and have a positive attitude towards therapy. It has also been claimed that psychoanalysis was of little benefit for patients with serious psychoses such as schizophrenia. With the advent of phenothiazines, schizophrenics are now better able to make use of insight therapies such as psychoanalysis.

Eysenck (1952) delivered the most damaging indictment of psychoanalysis when he reviewed studies of therapeutic outcomes for neurotic patients. He found that about half recovered within two years. What was so damning for psychoanalysis was that for similar patients who received no treatment at all (waiting list controls), the figure was about two thirds. Critics of Eysenck's findings discovered that he had made a number of arbitrary judgements about 'recoveries' that were unfavourable to the groups that received psychoanalytic treatments. Bergin (1971) found that by selecting different outcome criteria, improvement in the psychoanalytically treated group rose to 83% whilst the percentage of control group patients showing significant improvement dropped to 30%.

Eysenck's claims against the effectiveness of psychoanalysis showed the difficulties of evaluation in this area. Individual differences in patients and therapists, and the relationship between them, might confound attempts to measure the effectiveness of a particular type of treatment. Measuring the outcome of treatment may also present problems in defining what is meant by 'cure'. Corsini and Wedding (1995) claim that, depending on the criteria involved, estimates of 'cure' as a result of psychoanalysis range from 30% to 60%. Although changes in the occurrence of symptoms might be a suitable way of measuring the effectiveness of behaviourist techniques, the effectiveness of psychoanalytic therapy, which typically spans several years, is more subjective, measurable only by the extent to which the clients themselves feel that their condition has improved (Prentice, 1996).

Module Paper 6

Section A

1. Describe and evaluate constructivist and direct explanations of perception. (24 marks)

> **TIP**
>
> If you are following the AEB syllabus, this question is entirely predictable from the information provided in the syllabus. In the AEB syllabus, the word 'including' means that topics that follow this word can be specified in examination questions. You should make sure that you fully understand the terms used in the syllabus, whatever syllabus you are following, as these are the terms that will be used in examination questions. Thus, the AEB syllabus mentions 'constructivist and direct' theories of perception, and gives an example of each. You may well know these approaches better as 'top-down' and 'bottom-up' processing. Both approaches are required here, but only one theory would be required to illustrate each. The most popular theories for these approaches are Gregory (constructivist) and Gibson (direct), although others are also relevant. If you have trouble identifying which approach a particular theory belongs to, ask your teacher.

Perception is a combination of both the physiological processes involved within the senses and also the processes within the brain which integrate and interpret the sensory inputs from these systems. The two main explanations of perception prioritise the role of one or other of these different aspects of the perceptual process. Direct theories emphasise the importance of stimulus features in perception. In visual perception, for example, the visual information that reaches the eye is thought to contain sufficient unambiguous information about an object for effective perception to take place with little further processing. Gibson (1966) claimed that there is much more information potentially available in sensory stimulation than is generally realised.

Specifically, Gibson suggested that light reaching the eye does so in an 'optic array'. This provides information about such things as distance, movement and meaning. Interpretation is achieved through analysis of the information in this optic array by means of various cues (e.g. optic flow and texture density). The former of these can be illustrated by considering our movement towards some point on the horizon. The point towards which we move appears motionless, whereas the rest of the visual environment appears to move away from that point. The further away a point is from the horizon, the faster is its apparent speed of movement. Gibson also noticed that objects had a gradient of texture density as they moved from the near edge to the far edge. By 'picking up' this information from the optic array, observers are able to perceive some aspects of depth directly.

Gibson rejected the conventional view that we can perceive a meaningful environment because of the involvement of stored knowledge and experience. He claimed that the meaning of a stimulus is determined by the object's affordance, i.e. the physical structure of an object gives clues as to its potential use, therefore meaning is directly perceived. The particular affordances of an object that are detected by an observer depend both on the observer's species and also their current psychological state (Eysenck and Keane, 1990). Thus, a hungry person may well detect a different affordance for an object compared with someone who is not in the same motivational state. Eysenck and Keane suggest that Gibson's concept of affordance is a vital aspect of his theory. Without the notion of affordances, Gibson would have been forced to admit that the meaning of objects is stored in long-term memory rather than being directly perceived (Eysenck and Keane, 1990).

Gibson's theory has demonstrated that visual stimuli provide considerably more information than had been thought previously. His emphasis on the direct nature of perception has provided an explanation of the generally fast and accurate perception of the environment. Although, as Gibson suggests, the environment does provide us with a rich source of information, it seems unlikely that we use this in the simple, direct way proposed. Later theorists (e.g. Marr) cast doubt on the idea that perception could not require information processing from existing cognitive models. Gibson's theory also fails to provide an adequate explanation of why perception is often inaccurate. Although he claimed that the illusions used in experimental work constituted extremely artificial perceptual situations unlikely to be encountered in the real world, this dismissal could not realistically apply to all illusions.

An alternative view (the constructivist view) of the perceptual process sees the eventual product of our perception being 'constructed', that is built up from a combination of stimulus information, expectations and hypotheses. The perceptual process involves making sense of all the various bits of information provided by the senses. Perception is the end product of a process of which the stimulus is only one part. Hypotheses, expectations and previous experiences will interact with this stimulus to produce an inference about the external environment. A key aspect of this view of perception is that because of the role of hypotheses and expectation, perception will be frequently prone to error. Gregory (1970) has provided an explanation of how illusions can lead to perceptual error through the inappropriate application of previous knowledge to the stimulus given.

An illustration of how perceptual errors can occur was provided by Ittelson and Cantril (1954). They argued that if something appeared familiar but was actually novel, then perceptual hypotheses would be inaccurate. When viewing the Ames distorted room, subjects typically report that the room is of normal shape and size, even maintaining this belief when someone appears to dramatically grow and shrink as they move about within the room. According to Gregory (1970), many of the classic visual illusions can be explained by assuming that previous knowledge from the perception of three-dimensional objects is applied inappropriately to the perception of two-dimensional figures. For example, people typically see an object as retaining its physical size despite variations in retinal size as a result of changes in distance. Gregory argued that perceptual processing involving size constancy is applied wrongly to produce a variety of perceptual illusions.

If, as Gregory claims, perception is largely a matter of inference, then it would follow that perceptual processing would be more prone to error than it actually is. As with direct perception explanations, to place undue emphasis on one aspect of the perceptual process (i.e. either the stimulus or inference and hypothesis testing) does not appear to fit the facts. Gibson's answer to the problem of explaining illusions was to claim that laboratory studies are highly artificial situations that do not relate to the way in which we normally perceive. The fact that illusory stimuli tend to be presented only briefly lends some support to this claim. Brief presentations of stimuli prevent effective analysis and give more scope for interpretation on the basis of past experiences and expectations.

Neither direct nor constructivist theories seem capable of explaining all perception all of the time. Gibson's theory appears to be based on perceivers operating under ideal viewing conditions, where stimulus information is plentiful, and is available for a suitable period of time. Constructivist theories such as Gregory's have typically involved viewing under less than ideal conditions. Neisser (1976) has attempted to resolve this issue by suggesting that existing perceptual models guide us into sampling particular aspects of the stimulus environment. This tends to involve movement within that environment (a key aspect of Gibson's theory) as we gather information. During this stimulus exploration, if data gathered does not appear to match the relevant model, then the information in that model can be modified. Such a theory explains how constructivist and direct processes may be seen as interacting with each other to produce the best interpretation of the stimulus.

2. **Describe and evaluate experimental studies of selective (focused) attention.** (24 marks)

> **TIP**
>
> This is a frequently asked question that nearly always results in a great deal of inappropriate content. The major problem is that students seem unable to disentangle what is a *theory* of selective attention, and what are *experimental studies*. Quite often, students just stick down everything they know about selective attention without thinking about what is explicitly relevant to the question set. The question here uses the term 'selective attention' which is probably more familiar to most people, but the AEB syllabus uses the term 'focused attention' which is the same thing. Most work in this area has been on focused *auditory* attention, but focused *visual* attention is also on the AEB syllabus and can be asked.

Experimental investigations of selective attention usually involve a subject responding specifically to one stimulus from a presentation of more than one. Early research by Cherry (1953) used the binaural task, where two messages spoken by the same person were played to both ears at the same time. Typically, subjects found it very difficult to disentangle the messages if the only difference between them was one of meaning. Later research has tended to use a dichotic listening task where different messages are fed into each ear. Subjects are then required to shadow one message. Typically, subjects are unable to extract more than the most basic physical characteristics from the non-attended message.

Studies of selective attention have been generated by the many models explaining attention. Broadbent (1958) dichotically presented pairs of numbers to subjects' ears (one of each pair to each ear). If pairs of numbers were presented 4–6, 5–9, 2–7, they were recalled in the order 452697, demonstrating that each ear acted as a processing channel, and one channel operated at a time. Such research provided strong evidence for the existence of a single channel processor, but research by Underwood (1974) cast doubt on the validity of these conclusions. Underwood found that with subjects unused to the shadowing task, recall of material from the non-shadowed stimulus was extremely limited. However, when using subjects who were used to the shadowing task, recall of information from the non-shadowed stimulus was much higher. Other research (Allport et al., 1972) found that if the sensory modality of the incoming stimuli were different, then processing of both stimuli at the same time was much more likely.

Broadbent's central proposal was that unselected material would remain in a sensory buffer, where it would quickly decay. It would not, therefore, receive anything but the most rudimentary processing. Evidence from von Wright et al. (1975) challenged this assumption. They established that stimuli might be processed without conscious awareness. By pairing a word with an electric shock, and then presenting the word (without shock) in the unattended message, they produced GSR (Galvanic Skin Response) increases to the word without the subjects being aware of it.

Broadbent's theory clearly could not deal with the apparent processing of non-attended stimuli. Two alternative theories, those of Treisman, and Deutsch and Deutsch, provided explanations of how this might be possible. Treisman suggested that the unattended message was processed, but in an attenuated form. Deutsch and Deutsch proposed that a selective filter for processing did exist, but it was placed much further on in the processing sequence.

The implication of the Deutsch and Deutsch model is that all stimuli are processed, but only one stimulus leads to a response on the basis of its relevance or importance to a specific situation. Whilst the Deutsch and Deutsch explanation appears somewhat uneconomical, Eysenck and Keane (1992), point out that a model's lack of economy is insufficient cause for its rejection.

In an effort to resolve the problem of late versus early selection, Treisman and Geffen (1967) carried out research in which subjects shadowed one of two simultaneous messages, and at the same time monitored both messages in order to detect target words. Tapping would indicate detection. According to Treisman's theory, detection on the attenuated message would be less than on the shadowed message, whereas Deutsch and Deutsch's model would predict no difference in the detection rate. Treisman and Geffen found that the detection rate was much greater in the shadowed message than in the attenuated message, thus providing support for the early selection model rather than the late selection model.

Johnston and Heinz (1978) gave subjects a shadowing task in which target and non-target words were presented to both ears. In one condition, the non-target words were spoken in a female voice, and the target words in a male voice. In the other condition, both target and non-target words were spoken in the same male voice. Subjects were thus able to discriminate between target and non-target words early on in one condition (sex of voice) but not in the other. According to the Deutsch and Deutsch model, there should be no difference in the number of non-target words recalled in the two conditions (i.e. early selection would not take place). However, contrary to this position, the number of non-target words recalled was much lower in the condition where subjects were able to make an early discrimination about the target and non-target words. The conclusion from this and other similar studies is that selective attention is a more flexible process than previous theories had imagined. The amount of processing given to non-selected stimuli appears to be determined by the circumstances and task demands placed upon the processor.

Filter theories have been criticised by Neisser (1976) who claims that the laboratory investigation of selective attention typically only deals with what is *done* to a person rather than what a person actively *selects* from the stimuli. Neisser proposed that perception was a process of selecting from the information available rather than simply filtering out unwanted information. Benjafield (1992) concludes that contemporary research models no longer support the idea of a selective attentional filter. He suggests that people have a genuine ability to divide their attentional resources rather than switching rapidly back and forth between two tasks.

3. **Discuss applications of memory research.** (24 marks)

> **TIP**
>
> This is never a very popular question with students. That doesn't mean they avoid it, they just don't like it. Perhaps too many students gamble on studying only memory and then hope that the question set will be a nice general one on types of memory or forgetting. Of course life would be too easy if everything was predictable. Well, questions like this do appear and so you need to be prepared for them. Sometimes you are asked to include the research that these applications are based on, so the prudent student would be wise to revise this area thoroughly. Two other things worth mentioning here are the plural (applications means more than one) and the injunction 'discuss', which means that you are being asked not only to describe these applications, but also to evaluate them.

In 1978, Neisser argued that laboratory studies of memory were limited in coming to an understanding of memory processes. In one study, for example, Morris et al. (1985) presented football results to a group of students who had previously indicated, in a questionnaire, their knowledge of football. One group were given what they knew were real football results, whilst another group were given made-up results. For the first group, the correlation between recall of the real results and their knowledge of football was .82 whilst for the second group, the correlation between recall of the made up results and their knowledge of football was only .36. This study shows that the nature of the material used, whether real-life or artificial, made a considerable difference to the results obtained.

Findings such as these have led many psychologists to argue that in addition to examining memory in the laboratory, it is necessary to carry out research in real-life situations if we are going to be able to generalise to real-life memory (Gruneberg, 1998). This view has been attacked by Banaji and Crowder (1989) who argued that leaving the laboratory undermined the control of extraneous variables and therefore undermined the science of psychology.

Based on the idea of the schema in memory, Loftus (1979) has demonstrated how people's recall of events in simulated eyewitness testimony tasks is subject to distortions and inaccuracies due to the memory schema for the event described. Experiments have also shown how information presented *after* an event can influence the recall of the event. In one study (Loftus and Palmer, 1974), it was demonstrated that feeding misleading information to subjects had a dramatic effect on reducing the percentage of people who could correctly recall whether a car they had witnessed in an accident had passed a 'Stop' or a 'Yield' sign. Another study demonstrated that changing a question from 'Did you see *the*...' to 'Did you see *a*...' significantly affected the nature of recall.

Unfortunately it is difficult in these experiments to distinguish between *constructive* distortions, which occur when the person *encodes* the memory, and *reconstructive* distortions, which occur when the person retrieves it, and tries to fill in gaps in the schema. Other research on eyewitness testimony using the ideas of *encoding specificity* has discovered that eyewitnesses are considerably more accurate in their memory of events when they were able to recreate the context in which the event had taken place. For example, Wilkinson (1988) had young children taken back to a park where they had witnessed an incident, and found that this significantly increased recall. The experimental evidence of a large number of studies is that the 'cognitive interview' increases correct recall by about 40% without a significant increase in incorrect recall.

Mnemonics are devices for improving memory. The *method of loci*, for example, allows people to enhance their memory ability by the use of mental imagery. Specific memories are remembered by means of relating them to imagined locations. Other methods involve the learning of names through the association of a feature of the person to a distortion of their name such that the two appear connected. Using this technique, Morris et al. (1978) produced an 80% improvement in people's ability to put names to faces. Gruneberg (1997) has also used such imagery techniques to develop foreign language vocabulary courses. The evidence is that many learners can acquire a vocabulary of 350–400 words and a basic grammar in 10–12 hours. This contrasts with the average vocabulary picked up by British schoolchildren of 800 words in four years of schooling (Milton and Meara, 1998).

Mnemonic devices have a number of limitations. They do appear to help us learn lists of unrelated items, and also assist in everyday skills like learning names and faces. They do not, however, assist in the learning of complex material, and therefore must be seen as limited in their usefulness. On the other hand, a number of studies have shown that mnemonic devices can be highly motivating for adults and children in that they are perceived as being more enjoyable, faster and easier than conventional methods (Gruneberg and Morris, 1992).

Many patients suffer from an inability to remember medical advice. Ley (1978) based his laboratory investigations on earlier research on forgetting. Typically, patients remembered information based at the start of an interaction (primacy effect); information that was seen as more important by the patients, and information that was organised into categories rather than unorganised information. Another finding was that simple repetition of information had little impact on whether it was remembered. Using these findings, Levy made suggestions to the medical profession about how medical information might be communicated for better retention. The retention rate of patients following the new ideas rose from 55% to 70%.

4. **Describe and evaluate two theories of the relationship between language and thought.**

(24 marks)

> **TIP**
>
> This is a fairly straightforward question that invites you to demonstrate your descriptive and evaluative skills concerning two theories of language and thought. There are a number to choose from, although invariably one of these is nearly always Whorf's 'linguistic relativity hypothesis'. Students delight in reciting the story of Whorf's days as an insurance inspector, but it doesn't really get you any marks, so it is best avoid it. There are specific theories that attempt to explain this relationship, or at least show some aspects of it (as with Bernstein's theory described here), so you should not need to try and fit other theories (e.g. Chomsky) that are only tangentially related to the question. That is not to say that theorists such as Chomsky do not have anything to say about the language–thought relationship (Chomsky clearly does), but it would be up to you to explain exactly what this link is. You need to balance your theories and skills carefully in this answer to avoid running out of time.

The relationship between language and thought has been explained in a number of different ways, but the best known of these explanations was based on the view that language determined thought, and is known as the Whorfian hypothesis, after Whorf (1941), or sometimes the 'linguistic relativity hypothesis'. The central idea of this theory was that the language that a person speaks has a great influence on the way that they think and perceive. There is a weak and a strong version of the hypothesis. The weak version argues that language affects the way in which we perceive the world around us. The commonest example for this is the claim that Eskimos have many different words for snow simply because they are able to distinguish more types and characteristics of snow than we are.

The strong version of the linguistic relativity hypothesis proposes that any linguistic differences of different peoples are actually reflected in the ways they represent and think about the world. Hopi Indians and Thais do not, for example, have the same sense of past, present and future in their language as we have. This is seen as evidence for the rather different way in which they think about time. The assumption of this theory is that native speakers have a huge choice of words which allows them to perceive and remember specialised categories of objects in a way that is impossible for native speakers of other languages which lack the appropriate vocabulary (Willson, 1996).

Whorf's evidence does not support the conclusions that he drew (Newstead, 1995). Newstead claims the fact that there are differences in language and also in ways of thinking between Hopi Indians and English-speaking Americans does not indicate that language influences thought. He claims that it is not sufficient simply to look for linguistic differences between languages and assume that these reflect different ways of thinking. Evidence that Eskimos have more words for snow than we do is suggestive of this, but no more. Although there is little evidence to support the claims of the extreme version of the linguistic relativity hypothesis, there is some support for the weak form of this theory. Research by Carmichael et al. (1932) showed that verbal labels that were learned at the same time that subjects were shown ambiguous line drawings affected the recall for those drawings. However, such findings do not prove the Whorfian hypothesis. The fact that the type of label used can have an effect does not indicate that language determines thought, but rather that it helps in encoding. Newstead claims that a more tenable position is that language can affect the ease with which we process information. It thus seems reasonable to conclude that language can in some circumstances facilitate thought.

An alternative approach to the relationship between language and thought has been to consider the effects of social context on language. Bernstein (1962) suggested that children's language was influenced by their social environment. Of particular interest to Bernstein was the finding that the verbal intelligence scores of working-class children were typically inferior to their non-verbal intelligence scores. He drew a distinction between restricted code language and elaborated code, and claimed that the performance of children on tests of verbal intelligence (and ultimately school achievement) was mediated by their language code. Restricted code was characterised by fairly simple phrases which are readily understood in context, but less well understood out of context. The restricted code may be used as a shorter and more rapid form of communication between peers, and may rely heavily on shared meanings.

Married couples may frequently use the restricted code when conversing with each other because their shared experiences and understanding mean that it is unnecessary to spell out their meanings and intentions in great detail. By contrast, the elaborated code uses less direct and colloquial speech and is not context-specific. Sentences are more complex and contain less dependence on the context, so that the content can be more easily understood by another listener. Bernstein believed that the use of restricted code language disadvantaged those children who relied totally on it. Formal education, he believed, is conducted in the elaborated code, therefore children who could match their own language with that of the educational system were at an advantage.

Restricted code language may serve fairly well to support a mood, or to give a direct order, but it turns out to be awkward and inefficient when it must be used to convey precise information (Evans and McCandless, 1978). Bernstein did not, however, dismiss restricted code language as 'inferior', but described it as having 'directness and vitality'. There is some support for Bernstein's views. Hess and Shipman (1965) found that social-class differences do have an effect on children's intellectual development. They found that in many low-status families, language was used less to convey meaning, and more to give directions and commands to the child. While many studies have found social-class differences, many others have not (Higgins, 1976). The gross variable of social class may well mask other important social processes that affect communication style.

5. Discuss research into cross-cultural differences in child-rearing and the effects of such differences.
(24 marks)

> **TIP**
>
> If you are taking the AEB examination, you may remember that the term 'research' means knowledge derived from either empirical investigations *or* theories. Most of the research carried out in this area is empirical anyway, but there is always opportunity for the latter. There appears to be two different aspects of this question, although in practice it might be difficult to disentangle them. You should, however, try to include both in your answer. Our culture is one of the most profoundly important influences on our development and there is a surprisingly fertile research tradition in cross-cultural comparisons. Of course, the fact that there are cultural differences in child-rearing (e.g. between individualist and collectivist cultures) does not necessarily mean that children from those cultures grow up differently. It is up to you to describe research that has found differences in child-rearing practices and also the effects of those differences. Remember that you also have to evaluate the research, so don't get overwhelmed by the need to describe only differences. This is an area that invites subjective opinion, so do try to stick to the results of *psychological* (and perhaps sociological or anthropological) research rather than personal opinion. Occasionally, articles appear in psychological journals that are invaluable in the preparation of essay answers. One such article, by Professor Rudolph Schaffer, can be found in Volume 4, Issue 3 of *Psychology Review*.

The aim of a cross-cultural study is not only to examine the differences that exist between cultures with respect to child-rearing practices, but also to look at how people might be affected by the very different experiences that these cultures might provide. The cross-cultural study provides us with valuable information about child-rearing practices, extending the range well beyond that available in the West (Schaffer, 1998). It thus provides us with a natural experiment, and a means of examining the effects of some naturally occurring variable that differs between the chosen cultures. This enables psychologists to test predictions about the outcome of particular ways of treating children which, for practical and ethical reasons, could not be tested using more controlled methods of psychological investigation.

Consistent with other areas of social and developmental psychology, there has been considerable recent interest in the *context* in which behaviour occurs. This is seen as an important determinant of our behaviours, and therefore a constraint on any generalisations or claims to the universality of behaviour. The most pervasive of these contextual influences is the culture to which we belong. 'Culture' refers to the human part of the human-made part of a person's environment. It involves a set of rules, norms and customs that are agreed by the members of that group. As has become evident from cross-cultural research, what we find out about the behaviour of individuals in one culture may be specific to the cultural mores of that society and might well not apply to members of other cultures (Schaffer, 1997).

Different child-rearing practices may also reflect the economic conditions in which children are raised. The Gusii people, studied by LeVine et al. (1994) are a case in point. Gusii mothers keep all interactions with their children extremely brief. Everything they do is geared to soothing the baby rather than arousing it. The reason for this approach is that the mothers must return to working in the fields as soon as possible after the baby's birth, and then the baby will be handed over to the care of an older child. They must be sufficiently manageable for the older child (often no older than six) to cope. Thus, what goes on between mother and child is not a product of biological factors, but of cultural and therefore highly specific requirements.

Such findings may cause us to ask questions about the organisation of our own child-rearing practices. It can be argued (Messer and Messer, 1996) that the very notion of childhood is related to cultural assumptions about development. In many cultures, children are required to contribute to the income of the family from a very early age, either by tending animals or by being gainfully employed. In contrast, Western culture provides an extended period of childhood when offspring are educated and not expected to contribute to the financial economy of the family or the society. Indeed, whereas many cultures provide the opportunity for a clear 'rite of passage' from childhood into adulthood, Western cultures typically allow their children an extended 'moratorium' of adolescence where they may pass more gradually into the adult world.

Kagan and Klein (1973) studied children brought up in San Marcos, a small rural village in Guatemala. Throughout the first year of their life, infants in San Marcos are kept in conditions that would be described as gross deprivation in the West. The infants are passive and inactive, and rarely smile. This is very similar to the picture described for institutionalised children in the West, permanently damaged by their early treatment (Schaffer, 1998). However, when these children were examined between the ages of five and twelve, they showed no sign of any lasting damage in their mental capacities. The hypothesis that early deprivation permanently affects intellectual development was thus not confirmed, with cognitive development turning out to be far more resilient than was generally supposed (Schaffer, 1998).

A second area of interest to profit from cross-cultural comparisons of child-rearing practices has been concerned with the way in which children acquire language. It is generally held that early verbal experience is vital to develop the language system of the child. It would therefore follow, from this hypothesis, that children who do not have this experience will become linguistically retarded as a result. The Kaluli of Papua New Guinea, however, rarely talk to their infants as they regard them as having 'no understanding'. As a result, mothers tend to carry out the normal routines of early child-rearing in complete silence. However, Kaluli children become normal speakers of their language, with no sign that they have missed out on something essential to its development (Schieffelin and Ochs, 1983).

Within Western countries, differences in the school performance of children has frequently been linked to their socio-economic status (SES), which in turn has been linked to their sub-cultural background. There is evidence (Eggleston, 1985) that children from lower SES backgrounds are disadvantaged when faced with the unfamiliar culture of a middle-class school system, and as a result may not perform as well as less disadvantages children. It is difficult to interpret such differences. Not only is it unclear which aspects of their child-rearing experience have contributed to these differences, it is also unclear whether the differences actually exist at all, or whether the real difference lies more with the assessment and investigative methods being used.

The advantages of cross-cultural studies of child-rearing differences must also be considered in the context of their limitations. The vast majority of these studies, including the ones described in this essay, are not experimental studies, and therefore we cannot be sure whether there is a causal relationship between the differences in child-rearing practices and their presumed effects. It is possible that differences between cultures caused by genetic differences between cultures rather than differences in child-rearing practices. It is thus difficult to disentangle the effects of a specific socialisation experience from those caused by other factors of which we have little knowledge.

6. Describe and evaluate two theories of cognitive development. (24 marks)

> **TIP**
>
> At first sight, this appears to be a dream of a question: lots of opportunity to write about Piaget, Vygotsky, or perhaps Bruner – but wait... that's an awful lot of writing for 40 minutes. This is where you have to be strategic with your time, and where the 'eight paragraphs rule' will be your friend. If you have about 800–1000 words in total, that's 400–500 per theory, with half of that being for description and half for evaluation. It is so easy (and common) for answers to dwell far too long on a description of Piaget's stages, and then everything else gets crammed into 15 minutes at the end. Although most people refer to this as 'the Piaget question', it is worth pointing out that Piaget is not specified on the syllabus, therefore you can write about any theories that you like *provided they are relevant*. As always, when in doubt, ask your teacher.

Piaget claimed that cognitive development proceeded through distinct stages. In the first stage, the sensory motor stage, the child learns to coordinate its sensory input with its motor actions. At the beginning of this stage the child's behaviour is largely reflexive, but towards the end it is increasingly symbolic. The key development of this stage is object permanence, which develops when the child recognises that objects continue to exist even when there are out of sight. In the pre-operational stage, children's thought becomes increasingly symbolic, yet they are, as yet unable to conserve. In other words they are not aware that the physical properties of an object remain the same despite changes in its appearance. This, Piaget thought, was due to the child's reliance on perceptual rather than logical-based reasoning. They also display various 'curiosities' in their thinking; for example, egocentrism (the inability to take another's perspective) and irreversibility (the inability to envisage reversing an action).

In the concrete operational stage, children acquire the rudiments of logical reasoning, and display skills of reversibility, decentration and other skills of conservation. However, children in this stage can only solve problems if they apply to actual objects or events. They cannot solve problems when they are in the abstract. In the formal operational stage, children tend to reason in a more abstract, systematic and reflective way. They are more likely to use logic to reason out the possible consequences of each action before carrying it out.

Piaget also believed that a child developed as a result of two different influences: maturation, and interaction with the environment. The child develops mental structures (schemata) which enables him to solve problems in the environment. Adaptation is brought about by the processes of assimilation (solving new experiences using existing schemata) and accommodation (changing existing schemata in order to solve new experiences). The importance of this viewpoint is that the child is seen as an active participant in its own development rather than a passive recipient of either biological influences (maturation) or environmental stimulation.

Critics of Piaget have argued that his research studies underestimated the actual cognitive skills of young children. Using the three mountains experiment, Piaget demonstrated that children below the age of seven could not take the viewpoint of another person. Piaget discovered that children below this age are bound by the egocentric illusion; that is, they fail to understand that what they see is relative to their own position, and instead take it to represent the world as it really is. Hughes (1976) constructed an alternative test of egocentricity involving a policeman doll and a naughty boy doll which could be placed anywhere in the four quadrants made by two intersecting walls of a doll's house. Children below the age of five were able to place the naughty boy doll where he would not be seen by the policeman, thus demonstrating the ability to decentre. Donaldson (1978) explains this saying that it draws on the familiar game of hide and seek.

In Piaget's original research on the conservation of number, he discovered that pre-operational children were unable to understand that the number of objects in two rows remained the same even though their appearance changed. Piaget believed that the child was distracted by the fact that because the rows *looked* different, and neglected to take into consideration other features that would affect the outcome. By focusing only on the end results of conservation they see them as being unrelated rather than a transformation of one into the other. McGarrigle and Donaldson (1974) showed that children as young as four were able to conserve when the transformation was *accidental* (i.e. produced not by an adult experimenter but by a 'naughty teddy'). Moore and Fry (1986) demonstrated that children *were* distracted by the accidental transformation but only when there were a small number of coins. With larger numbers of coins they resorted to reporting *the way they look*, judging the longer row as having more coins (which is what Piaget originally claimed).

Vygotsky emphasised the role of the social environment in the cognitive development of the child. He believed that children are born with basic perceptual, attentional and memory abilities. These develop throughout the first two years of life as a result of direct contact with the environment. As children develop mental representation, particularly the skill of language, they start to communicate with themselves in much the same way as they would communicate with others. In Piaget's theory, this *egocentric* speech gradually disappears as children develop truly social speech, in which they monitor and adapt what they say to others. Vygotsky disagreed with this view, arguing that as language helps children to think about and control their behaviour, it is an important foundation for complex cognitive skills. As children get older, this self-directed speech becomes silent (or private) speech, referring to the inner dialogues that we have with ourselves as we plan and carry out activities.

Vygotsky believed that this private speech developed as a result of shared dialogues with adults and peers. If children can accomplish difficult tasks with the help of skilled others, then these dialogues become internalised within their private speech and are used in the future to guide their efforts in similar tasks. It is generally believed that these social dialogues have two important features. The first is *intersubjectivity*, where two individuals who might have different understandings of a task, arrive at a shared understanding by adjusting to the perspective of the other. The second feature is referred to as *scaffolding*. Adults may begin by direct instruction, but as children's mastery of a task increases, so the adult tends to withdraw their own contributions in recognition of the child's increasing success.

Research evidence (e.g. Berk, 1992) has tended to support Vygotsky's claim for the importance of inner speech. Children appear to use this type of speech more when tasks are difficult or when they unclear about their next moves. There is also evidence (Behrend et al., 1992) that those children who displayed the characteristic whispering and lip movements associated with private speech, when faced with a difficult task, were generally more attentive and successful than their 'quieter' classmates.

Unlike Piaget, who emphasised universal cognitive change (i.e. all children would go through the same sequence of cognitive development regardless of their cultural experiences), Vygotsky leads us to expect variable development depending on cultural diversity. In this way, Vygotsky places a greater emphasis on the role of *exogenous* factors in development, whereas Piaget stressed the importance of *endogenous* factors. The importance of scaffolding and language may not be the same for all cultures. Rogoff (1990) emphasises the importance of observation and practice in pre-industrial societies (e.g. learning to use a canoe among Micronesian Islanders).

7. **Describe and evaluate two theories of gender role development including the evidence on which they are based.** (24 marks)

> **TIP**
>
> This question illustrates two of the golden rules of the AEB syllabus. First, questions are set from the syllabus, and this is taken virtually word for word from that syllabus (note the important second part of the question sentence). Second, questions frequently specify the *number* of theories they require you to write about. This is rarely more than two, as such a request would invite rather superficial treatment of whatever number was requested. There are a number of theories (psychoanalytic theory and social learning theory, for example) that include gender role development as one of the outcomes of the more general process of socialisation. Make sure that your answer does not develop into a very general exposition of these two theories, only paying lip service to the development of gender. The second part of this question requires a description and evaluation of the *evidence* on which these theories are based. Although these theories are constantly being modified in the light of new evidence (which would be relevant here), try to include some evidence that is more original to the formulation of the theory. Remember that the 'Describe and evaluate' instruction applies to both the theory and the evidence, so the 'eight paragraphs rule' would be very valuable here.

According to social learning theory, gender role behaviours are acquired in one of two ways, either through reinforcement or through modelling. The best known study of the effects of differential reinforcement on gender role development was carried out by Maccoby and Jacklin in 1974. They reviewed a number of studies in this area and found little evidence that parents differentially reinforced boys and girls. Both sexes, it appeared were encouraged to be independent and discouraged from displaying dependent behaviour. Maccoby and Jacklin did find evidence for differential re-inforcement of specifically sex-typed behaviour, such as play with sex-typed toys, but played down the importance of toy use and interests in the development of gender role. A more recent analysis by Lytton and Romney (1991) provided support for Maccoby and Jacklin's major findings, but has highlighted the importance of toy use and activities as influential factors in gender role development. The provision of sex-typed toys and encouragement in their use is evident in a number of studies. A consistent finding is that parental interaction when playing is different when interacting with same-sex children than it is when interacting with opposite-sex children. Another consistent finding is that boys are more likely to be discouraged from engaging in feminine activities than girls part for engaging in masculine activities.

Block (1983) suggests that differential exposure and encouragement has far-reaching implications for the cognitive and personality development of the child. Boys have a greater opportunity to explore the physical world and therefore develop a sense of competence and mastery that is denied to girls. These findings show a clear relationship between parental response and gender role behaviour, yet this relationship is not as clear-cut as it may appear. It may well be the case that the parents are not causing the development of the gender-typed behaviour, but rather they are amplifying characteristics that are already there in the children. A number of studies (Snow, 1983; Lytton and Romney, 1991) have found evidence of behavioural differences between the sexes at a very early age. Research by Hines and Green (1990) has also demonstrated hormonal influences on behaviour, with the implication that males and females may be biologically predisposed to behave in certain ways.

More recent developments in social learning theory, however, changed this view of direct imitation of behaviour. Perry and Bussey (1979) proposed that in the real world, children observe the typical behaviours of many examples of both sexes. They notice those behaviours that are performed frequently by their own sex and infrequently by others. These abstractions of behaviour are then used as models for their own behaviours. Perry and Bussey supported this view with a series of experiments which demonstrated two major trends in the social learning process. First, they established that children notice the frequency with which behaviours are performed by the two sexes, and tend only to imitate those behaviours which are performed frequently by members of their own sex and infrequently by others. Second, if in an experimental situation some models behaved inconsistently, Perry and Bussey found that children would be more likely to imitate models that behaved consistently. In other words, they imitated those models whom they reasoned were good examples of their gender role. This finding, that children are more likely to imitate what they believe to be typical gender-appropriate behaviours appears to be the dominant underlying theme of the modelling explanation.

It is clear that modelling is a far more complex phenomenon than was originally thought. Contemporary social learning theorists emphasise the importance of cognitive factors in imitation. Children must have the ability to class males and females into distinct groups, to recognise similarities in their behaviour and to store those behaviours as abstractions in their memory in order to guide their own behaviour. It is this importance of cognitive reasoning in social learning that has extended our knowledge of gender role learning, yet the greater emphasis on cognitive functioning has brought the social learning theory closer to the next theoretical position, cognitive development theory.

In extending the early work of Piaget and applying it to the development of gender, Lawrence Kohlberg suggested that children must come to terms with the fact that gender is constant across time and situations, despite superficial changes in its appearance or manifestation. Kohlberg's theory of gender role development has three stages. The first occurs around the age of two, when children are able to consistently recognise themselves and others as either male or female, but bases this classification on physical appearance alone. This is the stage of gender identity. At the age of around two to three, children appreciate that gender is consistent over time. At this stage of gender stability however, children do not see that gender is stable across situations, believing instead that males may change into females if they engage in female activities. Around the age of five, children enter the stage of gender constancy in which they believe that gender is constant across time *and* situations.

There is research support for the stages proposed by Kohlberg but there is disagreement both about the ages at which they develop and about the relative importance of the three stages. Kohlberg believed that the most important acquisition was the development of gender constancy. He reasoned that if children did not have this they would be unable and perhaps unwilling to pursue gender appropriate activities. This has been explored in research such as that by Slaby and Frey (1975). These researchers established through interview the level of gender understanding of young children. They then showed them a split-screen videotape where they could watch either a child of their own sex or a child of the opposite sex. Apart from the finding that all children showed a tendency to watch the male model more than the female model, children's tendency to watch their own sex more was determined by their level of gender understanding predicted by Kohlberg's theory.

Some of Kohlberg's critics have suggested that he underestimated the importance of gender labelling; in other words the ability to recognise gender consistently and to divide the world on the basis of these labels. According to Fagot and Leinbach (1993) children will prefer gender-appropriate friends and activities almost as soon as they acquire the ability to label successfully. There is, however, wide variation in the age at which children can label. Fagot and Leinbach suggest that parents who give constant feedback, both negative and positive, on their children's gender-related behaviours produce earlier gender labelling in their children than parents who do not.

8. **Describe and evaluate research into the impact of life events in adulthood.** (24 marks)

> **TIP**
>
> This is a very friendly question (provided you know something about life events...) as it does not specify a particular number of life events. The essay is written to cover the eventuality that you might be asked to write about two, so has a dual use in that respect. A number of students attempt this sort of question when they clearly know nothing about research into life events. We all *think* we know a lot about this area, but are often surprised how difficult it is to sustain an intelligible answer for 40 minutes or so. Note also that the question asks for the effects of life events in *adulthood*, so, strictly speaking, the effects of divorce on children, or other trauma of childhood would not be relevant in this question. Inevitably most people write about the Holmes and Rahe social readjustment scale, but you do need to write about the *impact* of life events, not just the methods used in the investigation of this area. You are free to write about any life events you choose. No one can dictate what is a 'significant milestone' in another person's life. If it was David Batty missing *that* penalty that was significant for you, do feel free to write about it, but you won't find a lot of related research around (unless, of course, you know different).

A life event is a significant milestone or turning point in life to which we need to adjust and which will, consequently, have an effect on our personality (Wadeley, 1996). This classification would include events such as death of a spouse, divorce, retirement, and so on. Because of the potential for major adjustment as a direct result of these events, they are often referred to as 'critical' life events. Psychologists who subscribe to a 'life events model' of development see the changes in adulthood and old age as being largely a product of the critical events that we experience and the adjustments we make as a result of those events. Thus, developmental change in adulthood is seen as less smooth and continuous than might be proposed by lifespan theorists such as Erikson and Levinson.

Early models of life events saw these as representing pathological conditions which introduced stress into the person's life. In the Holmes and Rahe 'social readjustment rating scale', respondents indicate those events that they have experienced in the previous twelve months, and each is given a score for its potential stress to the person. The scale comprises 43 life events which are graded in terms of the amount of readjustment needed to accommodate to them. As a guide, marriage is given a stress score of 50 and death of a spouse the highest score of 100. The higher the score, the greater the likelihood of the person suffering some psychological health problem such as depression.

Evidence for the causal effects of life events on disorders such as depression is mixed. A key problem is the difficulty of knowing whether a person's health problems preceded or followed the life events in question. The fact that the two events are related is insufficient to infer that one has caused the other. There is also a tendency, following the onset of some major psychological problems, to enter a 'search for meaning', i.e. searching the memory for things that could explain the present state. Depressed patients are more likely to recall negative memories than positive memories.

Researchers have turned their attention to the effects of specific life events. The most severe of the Holmes and Rahe life events, loss of a spouse, has been described by Murray-Parkes (1972). In the first stage of grieving after bereavement, the initial response is one of shock, disbelief and extreme sorrow. The bereaved person then attempts to cope with the loss. They may turn to tranquillisers and sleeping pills and may show a number of physical and psychological symptoms. The intermediate phase is characterised by obsessional reviews and reminiscing about the deceased. In the recovery phase a more positive attitude may develop, with the person perhaps feeling that they have grown through the experience.

Research by Barrett (1978) has shown that men and women differ in their reactions to the death of a spouse. Barrett found that in a group of community residents aged 62 and over, widowers appeared to experience lower morale and greater dissatisfaction compared to widows. Evidence also suggests that older people adjust better and more rapidly to bereavement, although sudden bereavement produces the severest grief, whatever the age of the person who must deal with it. Sudden bereavement allows no chance for 'grief work' and the detachment to begin (Wadeley, 1996). The positive effects of this 'deathwatch' are not found in all studies. Research by Gerber et al. (1975) concluded that the period of preparatory grief made possible by long-term chronic illness did not have the positive effects predicted by other psychologists – in fact, it had a negative effect. Additionally, a study of 95 widows over the age of 55 found that those who expected the death of their husband, and those who engaged in discussions about funeral arrangements, financial arrangements, etc., adjusted no better, and in some cases worse, than widows who did not expect their husband's death or did not discuss plans before it (Hill et al., 1988).

Next to the death of a spouse, divorce is the single most difficult life event we are likely to face. Divorce is seen as a major stressor for both men and women, as it involves the loss of one's major attachment figure and source of emotional support (McIlveen and Gross, 1997). Bohannon (1970) has identified six stages in the divorce process (e.g. the emotional, legal and psychic divorce). Each of these stages may be accompanied by a conflicting range of emotions including pervasive feelings of failure, ambivalence toward the partner, grief, relief, loneliness and excitement (Wadeley, 1996). Both sexes tend to experience disorganisation during the first year after divorce, although there is some evidence (Chiriboga, 1982) that divorcees over the age of 50 find adjustment harder than younger people.

There is some evidence to suggest that divorce may have positive effects for women and their children. Woollett and Fuller (1996) describe how mothers who have been through a divorce often report experiencing a sense of achievement in their day-to-day activities. They have used the experience of divorce to develop a sense of mastery in their lives. Likewise, a study by Pearlin (1980) found that many couples experienced more distress during unsatisfactory marriages than they did after they divorced. Positive responses to divorce seem far more likely if the divorced person has a strong support network of friends and relations.

More recent views of the significance of life events have represented them more as processes than pathological events. Life events do indeed cause an initial reaction of shock and immobilisation, but individuals then have the chance to enter a new period of their life by building upon the experience in a positive and constructive way. Hopson (1981) describes seven phases of the transition cycle following a significant life event. These range from a state of immobilisation where there is a feeling of being overwhelmed by the event, through a stage of letting go, where the individual accepts the reality of what has happened and puts it behind them, to a stage of integration, when the life event might be integrated into their life rather than dominating it. Sugarman (1986) uses the example of a 'person with a disability', rather than a 'disabled person'. This developmental perspective is in contrast to the disease analogy of the Holmes and Rahe approach.

Module Paper 7

Section A

1. Discuss the importance of reductionism in explanations of human behaviour. (24 marks)

> **TIP**
>
> Questions in the *Perspectives* section of the AEB syllabus test your overview of the syllabus (this is known as 'synoptic' assessment). Thus, you should make sure that you draw your examples from at least two different sections of the syllabus (i.e. developmental psychology, comparative psychology and so on). There are also a number of different types of reductionism that you might write about, such as biological reductionism and environmental reductionism. You don't have to write about more than one type, but do remember the instruction to cover more than one section of the syllabus in your chosen examples. The injunctions used in the perspectives questions often invite a more discursive response (hence the use of the injunction 'discuss' in this question) than the more specific injunctions of, for example, 'describe and evaluate'. This is not a hard-and-fast rule, so do look out for other injunctions such as 'critically consider', and make sure that you know what they mean (see the Glossary on page v).

Reductionism in psychology refers to the concept of reducing behaviour into its component parts. Originally a theory put forward by Descartes in the seventeenth century, it argued that the mind was a completely separate entity from the body. Perceiving the body as a type of 'machine' meant that it could be studied in a very mechanistic way, and this led to the establishment of much of modern medicine. Psychology, likewise, has used this mechanistic philosophy in explaining human behaviour. The belief that human behaviour could be reduced to the action of chemicals, genes and learned habits dominated psychological thinking for much of the twentieth century.

There are three major areas in which the philosophy of reductionism has had its greatest impact – learning, psychopathology, and social behaviour. Watson's science of behaviourism was a major revolution in psychology. He argued that the mind was not a suitable subject for scientific study, and the only truly scientific approach was to keep to the study of things that could be objectively observed. Revolutions in other sciences (physics and atom theory, biology and cell theory) had been possible by the identification of small constituent units which made explanation of more complex phenomena more accessible. Watson considered that the same process would be possible in psychology, and identified stimulus-response links as the basic units of psychology. He emphasised the study of learning because that was the way that stimulus-response links were established. The reductionism of the behaviourists was challenged by the Gestalt psychologists. They argued that many aspects of human experience could not be broken down in this way, notably perceptual organisation and problem solving.

An example of the limitations of reductionism applied to perceptual organisation is demonstrated by the Necker Cube, where the same stimulus presented to the retina produces two different experiences. An attempt to explain this in terms of learned stimulus-response associations breaks down because the stimulus is identical in both perceived figures. Work on insight learning by Kohler (1925) demonstrated that learning often seems to take place by a sudden mental restructuring of the whole problem leading to rapid problem solving instead of trial and error attempts. Modern 'Neo-Behaviourists' have dropped the reductionist approach first proposed by Watson, and have adopted instead an interactionist approach, in which cognition *and* experience work together to produce particular behaviours.

In the field of psychopathology, the medical model of mental illness sees abnormality as being caused by a 'disruption' of biological processes in the brain. An example of this view can be seen in the medical explanation of schizophrenia. Kallman's (1938) twin studies appeared to show that schizophrenia ran in families, implicating inheritance as a causal influence of the disorder. Laing (1965) interpreted the family link somewhat differently. He showed how schizophrenics often came from deeply disturbed families, which he called 'schizophrenogenic'. The presence of a family member who could be classified as 'ill' in the eyes of the rest of the family led to a focusing of attention on the 'sick' family member, thus drawing attention away from the disturbed relationships in the rest of the family. For a complex psychological phenomenon such as schizophrenia, concentration on simpler genetic or chemical factors alone ignores all other levels of explanation which might also be relevant. Another example of the inadequacies of neurological reductionism can be seen in the role of motivation in recovery from cerebral strokes. Patients who are highly motivated tend to recover more quickly and more completely than those who accept their position passively.

A third area in which reductionism has been influential has been in the explanation of social behaviour. Following the publication of Wilson's (1975) book on Sociobiology, several attempts were made to explain *human* behaviour in terms of biological determinism. Altruism, for example, always a problem for biologists to explain, simply in that it did not appear to fit the Darwinian theory of natural selection, could now be explained in terms of 'kin selection' (Hamilton, 1964). Individuals tended to behave altruistically towards close relatives simply because they shared genes. According to sociobiologists, nature 'selects' certain psychological traits and social customs (such as kinship bonds and taboos against female adultery) because they help to ensure transmission of an individual's genes. More recent advocates of sociobiology (Dawkins, 1989) have tended to shy away from using sociobiological explanations as sole determinants of human behaviour. As some critics of genetic determinism point out, it makes little sense to dismiss human aggression on the grounds that 'we are innately aggressive', because such a statement does not provide explanation of 'peaceful' behaviour. By presenting such a static and predetermined view of human behaviour, it seems to reinforce the view that it is futile to try and change human nature, and as such appears to legitimise all manner of repressive social practices.

Throughout this discussion of reductionism, a recurrent criticism has been that the reductionist philosophy has ignored other equally legitimate levels of explanation. Traditional behaviourist doctrines, as outlined in Skinner's 'Beyond Freedom and Dignity' seem to imply that we are all pawns of our environments and advocate widescale manipulation by social and educational agencies. Kohn (1993) argues that this sort of 'pop' behaviourism distracts us from asking whether the behaviour being reinforced is worthwhile in the first place. Neurological explanations of abnormal behaviour advocate the use of drug treatments and institutionalisation as substitutes for real social reform. Genetic determinism, as presented in sociobiological explanations of behaviour, suggest that all manner of antisocial practices are understandable simply on the basis that they are 'natural', and even desirable, in the sense that they make the transmission of a particular gene line more likely.

It is the prerogative of the media, and even some academics, to seek simple, reductionist explanations for human behaviour. Unfortunately, this has the effect of distracting attention away from wider social questions, and may end up justifying existing practices which perhaps might be shown to be in serious need of change.

2. With reference to either psychological theory or research, discuss the view that such practices offer a gender-biased view of human behaviour. **(24 marks)**

> **TIP**
>
> This is a fairly wide question, but it does call for quite specialist knowledge, and as such should only be attempted if you really feel you know the area. You are being the opportunity to embed your answer in *either* theory or research, so you may choose to look at traditional theories (e.g. Freud, Kohlberg, etc.) or alternative theories (e.g. Gilligan, Bem, etc.) or even theories that represent a particular perspective on development (e.g. nature/nurture). Alternatively, you may discuss actual research strategies such as the problems of the experiment in investigations of gender difference and the 'turn to language' that is part of the post-modern revolution in psychology. This answer offers a combination of these two approaches. It would be wise to include at least two different theories if you are taking the former approach, and remember you are also being awarded marks for your critical evaluation of the material.

Gender bias refers to the treatment of men and women in psychological research and theory such as to offer a view that might not justifiably be seen as representing the characteristics of either one of these genders (Cardwell, 1996). One useful way of classifying gender biases in psychology is to represent them as either alpha biases or beta biases. Alpha biased theories are theories that see real differences between men and women, and may represent either an enhancement or undervaluing of one gender compared to the other. Many such theories offer a view of gender differences based on ideas of biological essentialism, treating all differences as though they follow logically and essentially from biological differences (Kitzinger, 1998). Beta biased theories tend to ignore or minimise differences between men and women. They have done this either by ignoring questions about the lives of women, or by assuming that findings from studies of males apply equally well to females.

Kohlberg's theory of moral development is typically seen as an example of an alpha bias theory that undervalues women, representing them as typically morally less developed than men. Gilligan's theory of moral development in women, on the other hand, is an example of an alpha bias theory that enhances women. The authors of these early theories have subsequently developed and elaborated their ideas, often criticising their own earlier studies in the process. The vast majority of psychological theories tend to lean more towards the beta bias because, in attempting to represent males and females in an objective and unbiased manner, they fail to represent the characteristics of one sex (usually women).

One theory that discovered consistent sex differences in moral reasoning was Kohlberg's theory of moral development (Kohlberg, 1976). When scored on Kohlbergian dilemmas, typical female responses that emphasised caring and personal relationships would merit a Stage 3 (mutual interpersonal expectations, relationships and interpersonal conformity) classification. This normally tended to place them at a lower level of moral reasoning than men who were often scored at Stage 5 (based on individual rights) or higher. Gilligan (1977) challenged Kohlberg's theory with the claim that women have a different moral voice, one based on an ethic of care and responsibility rather than the 'male' ethic of justice and rights. Gilligan claimed that this derived from a different sense of self, with males seen as separate individuals and women as being embedded in a web of relationships.

Critics of Gilligan's theory (e.g. Unger and Crawford, 1996) have argued that Gilligan's research (concerned with women making decisions about abortion) were not comparable with the rather more abstract dilemmas faced by Kohlberg's subjects. Gilligan was also accused of showing a failure to explore other factors than sex which could be related to differences in moral reasoning (e.g. social class, education, race/ethnicity). Finally, Gilligan failed to explore the possibility that what appeared to be a sex difference in moral reasoning might also reflect women's subordinate social position, with perhaps the ethic of 'care and responsibility' being expressed by less powerful people generally, rather than just women.

Kohlberg's theory may also be seen as an example of an androcentric bias, one which offers an interpretation of women based on the lives of men. Ideas of 'normal' behaviour may be drawn almost exclusively from studies of the development of males. Female development is often represented as a departure from this norm of male development, with the related inference that it is in some way 'abnormal' or 'pathological'. A well-known example of an androcentric theory is Freud's account of male identity development, in which the young boy's identification with his father leads to the formation of a superego and of high moral standards. Girls, on the other hand, who do not experience the same Oedipal conflict as boys, cannot, it appears, develop their superego (and thus their moral standards) to the same degree as boys (Cardwell, 1996).

Sandra Bem presented the concept of androgyny, which represented a type of gender-role identity where the person scores highly on both masculine and feminine personality characteristics (Bem, 1975). Critics (e.g. Unger and Crawford, 1996) have argued that personality variables such as androgyny do not correlate well with behaviour, with situational variables being far more important. Bem, like many other early writers in this area, has recently changed her view of what is important in gender role development. She is critical of the way in which psychology decontextualises everything, and is even critical of her own individualism which is expressed in the concept of androgyny. Bem argues that the concept of androgyny has been used at too private and personal a level, focusing on the person at the expense of the social situation and social organisation (Kitzinger, 1998). Like many other writers in psychology, Bem advocates a removal of the whole idea of gender polarisation, the exaggeration of gender differences, and the organisation of social life around them.

Questions about sex similarities and differences are not just scientific questions, they are also highly political (Kitzinger, 1997). Some of the answers to these questions have been used to exclude women from some occupations or to represent women as being victims of their own bodies. Menstruation has, in particular, captured the imagination of both scientists and feminists. The 'discovery' of pre-menstrual syndrome, during which female hormones become so unstable as to apparently render some women capable of murder, has led to a burgeoning of experimental research (Nicolson, 1997). Nicolson argues that many of the performance and mood differences traditionally identified between pre-menstrual women and others were products of poor research design. Several other well-designed studies, she claims, reporting no differences, were not published as their findings, being outside the existing paradigm, were subject to doubt.

Although psychologists are encouraged to develop a heightened awareness of human diversity in their writings and research investigations, this is not always in evidence. Howitt and Owusu-Bempah (1994) argue that white feminist psychologists, although dealing effectively with the issues of women, have failed to adequately address the issues relating to *black* women. In an analysis of American textbooks dealing with the psychology of women, Brown (1985) discovered that approximately one third were exclusionary (i.e. virtually no references to black women), one third tokenistic (making brief reference to black women) and one third segregationist (black women were represented only during references to the Third World). Howitt suggests that rather than being sensitive to black experience, textbooks on the psychology of women reproduce the non-feminist tradition in psychology texts, but against black people rather than women.

3. **Discuss the ethical issues of socially sensitive research.** (24 Marks)

> **TIP**
>
> This topic only appears in the AEB syllabus, and requires more than just an awareness of the BPS (British Psychological Society) ethical guidelines, which is what many students produce as a knee-jerk reaction to any question that has the word 'ethics' in it. The other thing that most people see as synonymous with the word 'ethics' (or in this case 'unethical') is the obedience research carried out by Stanley Milgram. Such research might be seen as socially sensitive, but it would be up to you to explain why rather than launching into an anti-Milgram tirade. Admittedly, this area is not as accessible or as well-known as the more straightforward topics on ethics, but there is plenty of useful material around that could be included. Reading the first sentence of this answer should give you some idea of what is and what is not 'socially sensitive'. An interesting consequence of the rather generous AEB interpretation of the word 'research' is that it covers all aspects of the research process (i.e. investigations, theory formulation and reporting). There are some important implications for the writers of textbooks and those who practise psychology. Some of these implications are included at the end of this essay. Note the use of the injunction 'discuss' which invites a more discursive treatment of the topic.

Research becomes socially sensitive when there are potential social consequences for the research participants themselves or for the class of individuals represented by the research (Sieber and Stanley, 1988). Sieber and Stanley have identified a number of ethical issues associated with socially sensitive research. The first concerns the reasons for the research being carried out. A number of research investigations have focused on aspects of human diversity such as homosexuality and race. Simply posing a research question such as 'Is homosexuality inherited?' or 'Are there racial differences in intelligence?' may have major social implications even if the research is never carried out. Such questions may be seen as potentially damaging to members of one sexual orientation or to one racial group by attempting to add some sort of scientific credibility to the prevailing prejudice (Sieber and Stanley, 1988).

Research into culturally sensitive issues such as gender and race may raise issues that to many are politically unpalatable, or which fail to take into consideration the needs and interests of the groups studied. In 1976, Scarr and Weinberg carried out a study of the effects of transracial adoption in the USA. They found that when black children were adopted by white, middle-class families, they showed significant increases in IQ and school achievement. Critics of this study claimed that the publication of these findings as well as the authors' interpretation of them failed to take into consideration the interests and perspectives of the groups studied, and as such was clearly derogatory to the black community.

A second important issue is the need to guard against the misuse of research findings. A controversial avenue of research in recent years has been to explore inter-racial differences in the achievement scores of blacks and whites, and sub-cultural differences between middle-class and working-class children. To explore cultural diversity in this way may have positive benefits for the groups concerned (perhaps leading to remedies for discovered differences, as in the Headstart programme of the 1960s) but may also be interpreted as supporting the idea of, for example, an inherited black inferiority. Research that identifies such differences between social and cultural groups can blind people to other possible explanations for the differences and can be used to support divisive discriminatory social policies (as demonstrated in Herrnstein and Murray's 'Bell Curve').

The development of ethical guidelines in psychological research may go some way toward making researchers sensitive to issues of social and cultural diversity, but may not deal effectively with all the possible ways of inflicting harm. Howitt (1991) points to the ambiguity of this position. Although it may not be seen as unethical to make claims concerning the genetic inferiority of a racial or gender group, it is likely to be unethical to deceive a member of that group about the purpose of a piece of research. Howitt believes that this narrow use of psychological ethics makes it a fairly ineffective way of guiding research into socially sensitive issues such as those relating to social and cultural diversity.

All ethical codes demonstrate a high regard for the well-being and dignity of research participants, but the codes of different professional organisations do show important differences that reflect the culturally important values of that country. The Canadian ethical code, for example, emphasises the 'dignity of persons' above all, with 'responsibility to society' being seen as less important when making decisions regarding the ethics of a research investigation. In the Slovenian code, there is a special requirement for psychologists to use the correct Slovene language in all written and verbal activities. Sensitivity to the importance of cultural identity through language is thus enshrined in all psychological investigations.

This sensitivity is also demonstrated through the decreased use of ethnomethodological research and the increased consultation with local religious and community leaders prior to a research investigation (APA guidelines, 1993). Ethnographic research, a form of undisguised participant observation has provided valuable insights into the social psychology of other cultures. Despite the fact that such observation is undisguised, there are important issues of privacy, particularly when individuals unintentionally reveal information they would prefer not to be recorded. This is particularly likely in informal contacts, when the researcher may be viewed as having stepped out of the formal researcher role. The presence of the researcher may also influence the behaviour of group members towards each other, affecting social relationships and even weakening the cohesion of the group being observed (Kimmel, 1995).

Although psychologists are encouraged to develop a heightened awareness of human diversity in their writings and research investigations, this is not always in evidence. Howitt and Owusu-Bempah (1994) argue that white feminist psychologists, although dealing effectively with the issues of women, have failed to adequately address the issues relating to *black* women. In an analysis of American textbooks dealing with the psychology of women, Brown (1985) discovered that approximately one third were exclusionary (i.e. virtually no references to black women), one third tokenistic (making brief reference to black women) and one third segregationist (black women represented only during references to the Third World). Howitt suggests that rather than being sensitive to black experience, textbooks on the psychology of women reproduce the non-feminist tradition in psychology texts, but against black people rather than women.

Research on racial differences is often carried out and its findings interpreted in ways which reinforce racist concepts and stereotypes about black people. Fernando (1989) believes that research projects involving black participants should take into account the effects of racism, both overt and covert, on the thinking and activities of the researchers. He claims that in Europe there is a lack of research orientated to the major concerns of black people, with ethical committees often misrepresenting researchers who conduct such investigations as being politically rather than psychologically motivated. Ballard (1979) claims that all psychologists have a moral responsibility to take into account the social and cultural worlds in which the research participants, and/or clients live. If they do not make such a response to cultural diversity, their practice is inadequate in practical and professional terms.

Section B

4. Medicine often throws up many innovative ways of helping people recover from surgery. One such technique popularised in recent years has been 'pet therapy' where patients are given regular access to dogs, rabbits and other small animals as part of the recuperation process following surgery. Psychologists studied children on two children's wards; one in a hospital that subscribed to the pet therapy scheme and one that did not. Results suggested that those children who were allowed regular contact with pets made a more rapid recovery after surgery compared to those who were not.

   (a) Explain one advantage and one disadvantage of natural experiments such as this.
   (4 marks)

   TIP

   You are being asked to 'explain' an advantage and a disadvantage of natural experiments such as this. What this means in practice is that you should 'show understanding of the topic through coherent and intelligible explanation'. It would be insufficient simply to identify an advantage and a disadvantage – you should say *why* it would be an advantage or disadvantage.

   - Because of the real-life context of studies such as this, they enable psychologists to explore issues of high natural interest that might have important practical implications.

   - As the experimenter has little control over the variables under study (e.g. the seriousness of surgery, the quality of nursing provision, etc.), any question of cause and effect is somewhat speculative.

   (b) Investigations involving children involve special ethical issues. Explain two ethical concerns that might apply to this study.
   (4 marks)

   TIP

   Don't use this as an opportunity simply to identify two ethical issues without linking them to this study. You should explain (see previous question) *specific* ethical concerns that might apply to *this* study.

   - One important ethical concern is informed consent. If the children are very young, or unable, for whatever reason, to make a reasoned decision about participation in the scheme, this can be made on their behalf. Thus, parents, or even members of the nursing staff acting 'in loco parentis' may make the decision on their behalf, providing the interests of the child are utmost at all times.

   - It is important to protect children from any psychological stress as a result of their participation in the scheme. If the child responded adversely to the presence of the animals, their exposure to them would immediately be terminated.

5. Psychologists were interested in the effects that music might have on workers carrying out simple computational tasks. They chose to study examination board script checkers, whose job it is to check that all the addition of marks is correct.

   In one room, script checkers completed two one-hour sessions of checking specially prepared scripts, the first in silence and the second with the accompaniment of piped music. In another room, a second group of script checkers, matched for age and experience with the first group, completed the same task, but in the reverse order (a process known as counterbalancing). Participants recorded all errors on a separate document, noting every time an addition error occurred.

The investigators awarded one mark for each script error correctly identified by the script checkers. The scores for the two groups are summarised in Figure 1.

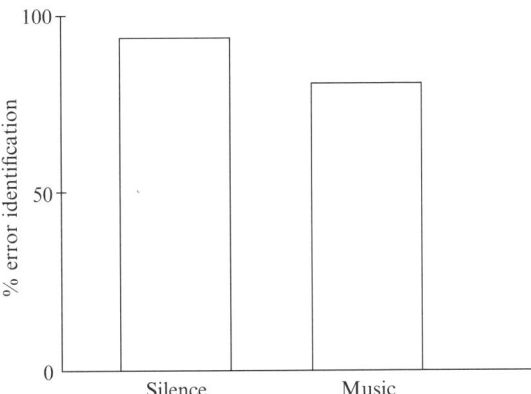

Figure 1: Summary of error identification scores for silence and music groups

A Wilcoxon signed ranks test was carried out on the data. The value of T (65) obtained was non-significant at the 5% significance level ($p > 0.05$), but significant at the 10% level ($p < 0.10$).

(a) State an appropriate non-directional (two-tailed) hypothesis for this investigation.

(2 marks)

> **TIP**
> Remember that all hypotheses should be *testable*, should make reference to operational variables (i.e. the specific variables being manipulated or measures), and in this case should not specify the direction of the effect being predicted. There is no need to include the word 'significant' in any hypotheses.

■ There is a difference in the number of administrative and addition errors detected by participants in the silence and music conditions.

(b) State the independent variable in this study. (1 mark)

> **TIP**
> This is a context-dependent question. It is not asking for the definition of an independent variable, but the identification of the independent variable in *this* study.

■ The presence or absence of music.

(c) Explain one factor relating to the choice of music that the investigators would need to consider when planning this study. (2 marks)

> **TIP**
> As this question uses the injunction 'explain' and offers two marks, you should both identify one factor and also say why this is so important.

■ It would be important to select music that isn't too specialist as some participants would like it and others might not. This would lead to it being a pleasant accompaniment for some participants, but an unpleasant distraction for others.

(d) **The investigators chose a matched-participants design for this study. Describe one advantage of this method.** (2 marks)

> **TIP**
> As there are two marks for this question, it is fair to assume that one mark would be given for a partially correct or brief answer, and two marks for an answer that was developed within the context of this particular answer. In the AEB syllabus, one mark equals almost two minutes, so take your time and earn all the marks available for a question.

■ One advantage of the matched-participants design is that it minimises the effect of important participant variables that might otherwise affect performance across the two conditions. In this study, more experienced script checkers may also be more accurate, therefore it is important to match participants in terms of this.

(e) **Explain the purpose of counterbalancing in this investigation.** (2 marks)

> **TIP**
> Note the words 'explain' (see previous questions for advice on this) and 'this' which means you are being asked why counterbalancing was used in *this* investigation, not why it is used in investigations in general.

■ Counterbalancing is used in this study to minimise the effects of order on error identification. Participants may become fatigued over time, and their accuracy rate may drop. Changing the order of conditions minimises this effect across the two groups.

(f) **Name the graphical technique shown in Figure 1.** (1 mark)

> **TIP**
> A nice simple question, worth only one mark, so just the words 'bar chart' will get you the mark. Go for it!

■ Bar chart.

(g) **Give three reasons why the Wilcoxon signed ranks test was used for this investigation.** (3 marks)

> **TIP**
> This would be very straightforward if you have used a Wilcoxon test in your coursework. If you haven't, remember these are very common questions in AEB examinations, so make sure you can give three reasons for using all the tests on the syllabus. Note that you are being asked specifically to say why the Wilcoxon test was used in *this* investigation. Don't write down all the possible reasons you can think of, in the hope that three of them will be right: the first three will be marked and subsequent reasons will be ignored.

- It is a test of difference, and performance was being tested between two conditions (silence versus music).

- It is used with related designs as with the matched-participants' design used here.

- It is used with data that is at least ordinal. The data in this study is ratio but is converted to ordinal data for the purposes of test calculation.

   (h) **Explain what is meant by the statement 'The value of T (65) obtained was non-significant at the 5% significance level ($p > 0.05$), but significant at the 10% level ($p < 0.10$).'**

   (3 marks)

> **TIP**
>
> It is very easy to get tongue-tied with questions like this. Think very carefully before answering. When you get a significant result, that tells you how likely you are to get a particular set of results if the null hypothesis for the investigation was actually true. If you get a result at the 5% significance level, it seems unlikely that you would have found such a difference (in this investigation) if the null hypothesis really were true. However, you didn't make the 5% level, and the 10% level leaves you undecided whether the null hypothesis had actually got it right. Better safe than sorry, so the null hypothesis would be retained. These questions are very common, and can be quite complicated to get right, so ask your teacher to explain the concept of significance to you and then be prepared to use it within the context of a specific investigation. Note that in the Wilcoxon test, as with certain other statistical tests, the calculated value should be *less* than the critical value, not more as in most tests.

- The calculated value of T was less than the critical value at the 10% significance level, but exceeded the critical value at the 5% level. The probability of obtaining these results if the null hypothesis was true was therefore less than 1 in 10, but greater than 1 in 20 which is the normal minimum level of significance necessary for rejection of the null hypothesis.